# budget
# family
# food

Rebecca Wilson

# *budget*
# family
# food

**Delicious money-saving meals for all the family**

# Contents

# Hello,

Welcome to *Budget Family Food*. I'm really excited to share this book with you – it's been created to give you guidance on cooking and eating with your family without breaking the bank. All the recipes in this book have been created budget consciously, using thrifty ingredients and clever cost-saving swaps.

Weaning and feeding little ones especially can be quite expensive, trying to ensure you give them a balanced meal and a wide variety to help curb any fussiness that may develop. These recipes have been created using a wide range of readily available ingredients found in most supermarkets for a relatively low cost compared to other alternatives.

The way I like to run my kitchen is to keep my pantry stocked with fairly inexpensive items, so I can use these to make an array of dishes simply with them, or by adding a few extra ingredients to my shopping list. You can find my pantry list on page 30, and each recipe states which items will be from the pantry, and which extra items to add to your weekly shop. This helps to keep the cost down, by avoiding needing to buy a large amount of ingredients for every meal you plan to cook.

You can find lots of tips and tricks for shopping and feeding your family on a budget too.

I hope you find this book useful.

Lots of love,

Rebecca
X

# Cooking
## for all
## the family

Cumberland Pie
(see pages 151–152)

# Eating with our babies and children

Studies show that eating with your child raises confident little eaters for many reasons. Our children watch us and naturally want to copy what we do, so by showing them how enjoyable, easy and exciting eating healthy food can be, our little ones are more likely to be a little less picky with certain foods and be more open to trying new ones. Not only will modelling how you physically eat food and the motions of chewing, drinking and using cutlery help your baby learn how to wean onto solid food, but as they grow a little older it will minimize fussy tendencies. And the best bit – you only need to cook once, making feeding your family that much easier!

## How to cut and serve the food in this book

To make these meals suitable for our tiniest of taste testers, we need to cut and serve the food in an appropriate shape so it's easy for them to pick up and feed themselves, ultimately making it safe for them to eat. The aim is to cut most foods into finger strips so that little fingers can grasp the food easily. Foods like small patties, which a baby may be able to hold easily, can be left whole for them to hold and take a bite of. Food that babies can take bites of is usually safer for them to eat than food that's cut into bite-sized pieces. By allowing your baby to take a bite of the food themselves, not only are they developing this important skill, but they are determining how much they can handle, which reduces the risk of choking. Foods that are a choking hazard when whole must be cut to a smaller size to be safe to serve to little ones. Here's a few examples of common foods and how to serve them:

**Citrus fruits** – Peel whole and cut in half widthways, keeping the segments still attached. Baby will be able to pick up the whole fruit and eat from the cut side, which now mashes easily in their mouth.

**Banana** – Tear into finger strips down the centre of the banana (using your finger to separate into three strips).

**Toast** – Butter or top with mashed fruit or yogurt to soften a little, then cut into finger strips.

**Hard-boiled egg** – Peel and cut into quarters, lengthways.

**Peas, sweetcorn and pomegranate seeds** – These can be served whole as they are too small to pose a choking risk. Corn on the cob can be served cut into 5cm (2in) rounds so it's easy for little ones to pick up.

# The important bits

## A note on choking

Many parents are understandably extremely worried about their baby choking when serving solid food. It is something you must take seriously as there is a risk there. However, it is also equally really important to avoid letting this worry stop you from serving a variety of foods to your baby. You may unintentionally restrict their diet or prevent them from developing their eating skills by holding back from offering finger foods. It's important to also note that there is no greater risk of choking when offering finger foods to baby vs just purées. I recommend taking a first aid course if you can or researching baby first aid, including CPR, before you start weaning so you feel confident if the worst case happens. Do be reassured that it is rare for babies to choke, but it is still important to be very vigilant, just in case. Here's a few steps you can take to lessen the risk:

- Do not leave baby alone when eating.

- Ensure baby is developmentally ready to start eating (see page 15).

- Always serve food in a safe way – see foods to avoid on pages 12–13.

- Make sure they are in an upright sitting position, ideally in a high chair with a foot rest and not on your lap.

- Avoid serving food in walkers or bouncers as the sudden movements can be dangerous.

## Gagging vs choking

When you begin to offer solid food to baby, they're likely to experience gagging in those first few months. This is very different to choking, and normal for baby to do. Gagging will be noisy, as baby is not used to solid food being in certain places in their mouth. When gagging, baby will be visibly trying to change the location of the food, bringing it forward from the back of their mouth; baby's face will also likely darken in colour. If baby is coughing and making grunting noises, and can still be seen to be breathing, this is gagging and very normal. Intervention is not needed and it can often be more dangerous if you try to remove the food yourself, which can lead to choking. Be vigilant and ready to help if choking begins, but allow baby to fix the gagging problem themselves. It is important they learn how to resolve this problem – however difficult it is for us adults to watch.

In contrast, choking is when an object is lodged in baby's throat and blocking their airways. When choking, baby will be making very little noise; they are not breathing, with their chest pulled in as they struggle to take breath. Baby's face may also become paler in colour. Act immediately – quickly remove them from the high chair, patting them on the back with baby leaning forward and following the baby CPR process. This part may seem scary but it really is just a safety precaution, try not to let it take the fun and joy out of feeding your family.

## Got no teeth?

It is a common misconception that babies need teeth to eat finger foods. In fact, their gums are hard enough to chew and process food from 6 months of age. Some babies do not grow their first teeth until they are over a year old, and in most cases the back molars (chewing teeth) usually do not come in until little ones are around 18 months old plus. This would be too long to wait to serve finger foods, and you run the risk of delaying their opportunity to develop their eating skills.

## Salt and sugar

Every recipe in this book can be served to every member of your family, including babies from the age of 6 months. The recipes have been specifically developed to be low in salt and sugar so that they are safe for little ones to enjoy, but still delicious for us adults too. (Specific instructions are included on recipes where moderation for babies is advised.) The use of salt, and seasoning our own food as adults, is an act that is learnt and developed as we grow older, therefore not everyone has the same salt tolerance, and some people may wish to have a little more seasoning on their plate. Please do feel free to season your own food once the family meal has been dished up, or your little one's portion has been removed from the pan. Adapt recipes with extra chilli, pepper, sugar or spice if you feel like it too. Make your food your own, it's there to be enjoyed!

**Salt intake guide:**

- Babies under 12 months should have less than 1g salt per day (0.4g sodium).

- Toddlers aged 1–3 years can have a maximum of 2g salt per day (0.8g sodium).

- Children aged 4–6 years can have 3g salt a day (1.2g sodium).

- Children aged 7–10 years can have a maximum of 5g salt per day (2g sodium).

- Children aged 11 years to adulthood can have a maximum of 6g salt per day (2.4g sodium).

# Foods to avoid serving to little ones

**SUGAR –** Try to avoid too many sugary treats for little ones, as over-exposure to sweet tastes can lead to a preference for sugary flavours, in particular in the first few years of weaning. This also includes naturally occurring sugars in foods like fresh fruit juices, as it can lead to tooth decay. I have developed these recipes to be lower in sugar, and where possible tried to use sugar derived from more natural sources, such as those naturally occurring in fruit. If a recipe requires a fruit purée pouch, this is simply an unsweetened 100%-fruit baby purée pouch found in the baby food aisle. Be sure to use one which has no added cereals, and try to opt for a sweet flavour like apple or mango, but it's no problem if there is a mix.

**SATURATED FAT –** Babies and young children need lots of fat in their diet as they are using lots of energy growing, learning and being active, so choose full-fat versions of dairy products like milk or cheese until they are 1 year old. From then on you can swap to semi-skimmed milk if you wish. However, do be mindful to limit your child's intake of saturated fat in foods like cakes, biscuits (cookies) and crisps (chips).

**WHOLE NUTS –** Avoid serving whole nuts and peanuts to babies and children under the age of 5 years as they are a choking hazard. Chunky or thick nut butters can also pose a choking risk. Smooth nut butters, crushed and ground nuts can be served to baby from around the age of 6 months.

**RAW EGGS –** From 6 months you can serve eggs to baby. In the UK, choose hen's eggs that have the British Lion quality stamp on them, which are safe to serve raw as an ingredient in food like homemade mayonnaise, or lightly cooked like a soft-boiled egg.

If the eggs are not British Lion stamped or you are in doubt, always fully cook the white and yolk of the egg until they are solid before serving to baby. This also includes duck, goose or quail's eggs.

**HONEY –** Honey can contain bacteria that can produce toxins in baby's intestines leading to infant botulism, which is a very serious illness. Avoid serving honey to babies under the age of 12 months. This also applies to honey that has been used as an ingredient and cooked, as the risk still remains. This includes shop-bought products that contain honey in the ingredients, so always read the packaging.

**CERTAIN CHEESES –** Cheese is packed full of calcium, protein and vitamins, making it a fantastic food to serve to babies and young children as part of a varied diet. However, it is advised to offer only pasteurized full-fat cheese from the age of 6 months. This includes hard cheese, like Cheddar, cottage cheese and soft cream cheese.

There is a risk of the bacteria listeria in soft cheese like Brie, Camembert, ripened goat's cheese, blue cheese or cheese made from unpasteurized milk. Listeria can make baby feel very ill so it's best to avoid. However, you can use these cheeses to cook with, as the listeria is killed when cooking.

**RICE DRINKS –** Babies and young children up to the age of 5 years shouldn't drink rice-based drinks, especially not as a replacement for breast or formula milk, as it contains high levels of arsenic. Babies are fine to eat rice in the EU, as the levels are monitored for rice and rice-based products. If outside the EU, check with your national health service guidelines for advice.

**RAW SHELLFISH –** Always fully cook shellfish such as mussels, oysters, clams and cockles to avoid the risk of food poisoning.

**SHARK, SWORDFISH AND MARLIN –** Avoid shark, swordfish or marlin as the high levels of mercury found in them can affect the development of baby's nervous system.

## Let's talk veggies

It can be very tricky to get your kids to love vegetables. The trick here is to keep offering consistently from the moment you begin weaning. I know it can be tempting to avoid offering foods you feel they will refuse, especially when you don't want anything to go to waste. Always model yourself eating the same food, and be consistent with how often you're serving foods you feel may be rejected.

You can hide veggies in recipes, and many of my recipes do this to ramp up the nutritional value of the meal. However, to allow our little ones to get used to eating veggies, it's important to be honest with them about what ingredients are in the meal, especially when they enjoy it, as it allows them to become more comfortable with that food. Try to serve veggies on the side of main meals too, even if the dish has vegetables inside, but this doesn't have to be a hard and fast rule. It is important for little ones to be exposed to veggies in their whole form on a regular basis to help them overcome any potential fussiness.

# First foods

Every recipe in this book is suitable for all ages, from us adults to older siblings and, in particular, babies from the age of 6 months. Therefore you can wean your baby using the recipes within this book, while also feeding the whole family. Before you get started, let me guide you through some of the most common questions I get asked about offering first foods to baby.

## Equipment needed for baby feeding

As your baby is coming up to weaning age and about to enjoy their first tastes of solid food, thankfully there isn't an endless list of items you'll need, but there are a few key pieces that will make the transition to eating solid food safer and easier:

- A straight-back highchair with a safety harness, with a large tray or the ability to sit close to the family dinner table. If the highchair has shoulder straps, ensure they aren't so tight that baby is leaning back, and cannot bring themselves forward. If baby was to gag on a piece of food, we want them to be able to lean forward to dislodge the item themselves. An obvious note but one to remember – do ensure you never leave baby unattended when they are eating.

- Use soft weaning utensils at first, ideally firm silicone or a flexible plastic, which is kinder on baby's gums than metal spoons. And as you progress with weaning, you can let baby use a soft-grip metal toddler spoon and fork to help them try to feed themselves using cutlery.

- A good catcher or long-sleeve bib. I always liked to layer these two with the long-sleeve bib underneath to save baby's clothes, and the silicone catcher bib on top to minimize food waste.

- A small open or valve-free sippy cup. It's a good idea to allow baby to practise their drinking skills from the beginning of weaning so they learn this useful ability from an early age. Until 12 months old, babies don't need additional hydration, their breast or formula milk will be enough. This is mostly just for practice so that when they begin to reduce milk feeds they have the skills to take hydration in other ways.

- Small, child-friendly bowl and plate, preferably with good suction underneath to attach it to the table and minimize food waste.

- Storage boxes for the fridge and freezer, and non-stick baking paper and foil to store leftovers.

### Is my baby ready for solid food?

There's a few factors to consider here when assessing whether your baby is ready for solid food. It is often a misconception that baby is ready when they are waking more in the night, chewing on their fists as this is usually a teething or developmental trait, watching you eat intently, or wanting extra milk feeds. These are all normal and usual behavioural milestones which all babies follow around the same age of weaning, however these are not signs to tell you that baby is ready to eat. Instead look out for the following:

- Baby will be around the age of 6 months, as this age is generally when baby's body is developed enough to digest and process solid food.

- Your baby will be able to coordinate their eyes, hands and mouth to see food, pick it up and bring it to their mouth.

- Baby will be able to stay in an upright sitting position and able to maintain good head control for at least a minute, unaided, without leaning on you or another object. This is important to minimize the risk of choking.

- Baby's tongue-thrust reflex has lessened and they will be able to swallow food, rather than spit it out. If baby pushes their tongue forward naturally and spits out all their food, wait a couple of days and try again, this motion will go soon.

### Should I do baby-led weaning or spoon-feeding?

Firstly, let me explain what the difference is. Baby-led weaning, or simply finger foods as I like to call it, is when you offer your baby whole solid food and allow baby to independently pick up food and feed themselves. This helps little ones to learn the process of eating at a quicker pace, and introduces baby to a larger variety of foods visually, texturally and flavourfully, which in turn can lead to a confident eater. Spoon-feeding baby purées on the other hand is where you purée baby's meals with a little milk or water (these can be any of the recipes in this book so you're still able to eat together as a family) and feed baby using a spoon. This way is often used as it may feel more manageable and familiar to both baby and parent. It is important to note, if you decide to use this route, that the consistency of baby's purée should increase in texture within a couple of days of starting to wean baby, with the goal to be offering very coarsely lumpy bowls of food by the time baby is 10/11 months old. Then you can transition to finger foods around the time of baby's first birthday.

My favourite way is to wean baby with both methods. From the age of 6 months, offer a few pieces of finger food, alongside that same food puréed for the first 2–6 weeks to ease baby into eating solid food. This allows them to taste the same flavour in a variety of ways. Remember the goal of weaning is to teach baby how to eat, not to feed them until they are full. Up until baby is 12 months, they will be getting the majority of their nutrition from their breast and/or formula milk. Offering a wide variety of foods for a healthy balanced diet is important to not only minimize fussiness, but also to help baby learn how to eat, along with ensuring they are digesting a good variety of essential nutrients and vitamins. Up until 12 months, the main aim is to teach baby how to eat, so try not to worry too much about whether they have eaten a certain amount or not. Right now it's all about practice and learning the physical motions of eating and getting baby used to a wide variety of foods, so that when they do need to rely on solid food for their main nutrition, they have the skills and the desire to eat a healthy balanced diet.

## How to start

Initially it's best to ease baby into solid food for the first 1–2 weeks. Starting with vegetables, soft steam and/or purée can support baby to learn about more bitter tastes. Up until 6 months, baby has only tasted their comforting and sweet-flavoured milk. In those first few days, it will be helpful in the long run to get baby used to solid food tasting different to this sweet flavour they are so used to. You may experience a few funny faces or unsure responses. This doesn't mean that baby doesn't like it, it simply tells us that it's new and they are trying to figure it all out, so it's important that we don't presume baby doesn't like that flavour, then avoid serving again, as unintentionally we will be restricting their diet and making it harder for baby to learn to love that food in the long run. This same method can be approached with a little one who is older and refusing certain foods – keep offering on a regular basis, it can take up to 20 times of offering a food for a little one to learn to love it.

Cauli and Broccoli Cheese Soup with Garlic Toast (see page 181)

### How to cook vegetables for baby's first tastes

Place a medium to large saucepan over a high heat, half-filled with boiling water from the kettle. Use a steamer attachment with a lid, or a metal colander placed over the pan and a large lid on top to act as a makeshift steamer. Steaming helps lock in all the nutrients and is the healthiest way to cook vegetables for newly weaning babies. Wash and peel the veg, if necessary, then cut into the appropriate shape for baby. You simply need it to be an easy size and shape for baby to be able to pick up the food easily independently.

Here's a few examples – these are really rough guides to help if you're unsure and there's no need to get the ruler out. For more on how to serve food to baby, see pages 14–16.

- **Root veg like carrots and parsnips** – Peel and cut into approx. 2cm (¾in) wide and 7cm (2¾in) long batons. Steam for 12–15 minutes until soft.

- **Broccoli** – Cut into medium florets and steam for around 6 minutes until tender.

- **Green beans** – Strip woody ends and steam for around 7 minutes.

- **Courgette (zucchini)** – Cut into batons as above and steam for around 6 minutes.

This veg can be the same vegetables that you are eating with your meal so you're only cooking once, and baby is learning how to eat while watching you. Once you have mastered veggies, move on to soft fruits like bananas, soft nectarine wedges, quartered or large whole strawberries etc. After a week or so, if you feel confident to move on to the next stage of weaning, you can try any of the recipes in this book. It may seem daunting at first, but don't worry. It's really great to offer baby a wide variety of flavours and textures, this way they will learn much easier. And they will be able to handle much more than you expect them to. Remember, baby doesn't need any teeth to chew, their gums are hard enough.

## Which meal is best at the beginning?

This really depends on your family's and baby's schedule. Find a time when baby is happy, not too hungry, but also importantly not too full from their last milk feed. Ideally around half an hour before their next scheduled milk feed, so that you can offer milk after the feeding session is over. If you can, time it so that you eat your meal alongside baby too, which will really help – see page 9 for why.

# Adapting the recipes to suit your diet

If you have specific dietary requirements, whether dairy-free, gluten-free, egg-free, vegan or vegetarian, there are ways to adapt the recipes in this book to suit your family's needs. Look out for the * symbol next to the ingredients in the recipes to see which ones you can substitute. Here I have listed some foods that you can use as substitutes – unless it is specifically stated in the recipe, choose whichever one works best for you. And always check product packets for hidden ingredients that you may not be aware of.

## Dairy-free cooking

**BUTTER –** For most recipes, you can replace butter with dairy-free spreads (these are better for baking), or with coconut or olive oil.

**MILK –** You can substitute milk for plant-based alternatives in all recipes. Soy, pea and oat milks are all a suitable swap from 6 months onwards, and you can introduce nut milks for children over 2 years old. However, avoid substituting with rice milk as this is not suitable for children under the age of 5 years. Try to choose a milk alternative that is fortified with extra vitamins to ramp up your nutritional intake.

## Dietary Requirements

Look out for these icons accompanying each recipe to find out if it suits your dietary requirements. Whenever you see a * next to the letters in the dietary icon, this indicates that the recipe can be adapted to suit this dietary requirement. Please take care and turn to this section for possible alternatives to the ingredients listed.

GF  Gluten free

EF  Egg free

DF  Dairy free

V  Vegetarian

Vg  Vegan

**DISCLAIMER** Those following strict allergen diets should always check the packet for guidance about suitability.

**CHEESE –** There are many dairy-free cheeses on the market these days, shop around and find ones that you like the taste of and melt well. It is best to choose a cheese alternative that is fortified with B12 and other vitamins, if possible. Alternatively, in most recipes you can just leave out the cheese or swap it for nutritional yeast flakes (about 1 tablespoon replaces 40–50g/1½ –1¾oz of cheese), however, be mindful that in both cases this may reduce a little of the moisture content in the finished dish.

**DAIRY CREAM, CREAM CHEESE AND YOGURT –** You will find plant-based alternatives to these products in most supermarkets. If you do struggle to find anything, use an alternative that is a similar texture to what you are trying to replace. For example, you could replace Greek yogurt with plant-based yogurt or plant-based cream cheese thinned down with a little plant-based milk. Don't be afraid to experiment and make the recipe suit you.

## Egg-free cooking

If egg is the main ingredient in a recipe, for example in an omelette, it is not always possible to replace with an alternative option and so it may be best to choose another recipe in this case. However, when egg is used to bind ingredients together, such as for pancakes, flax and chia eggs are a great substitute. Be mindful that they do not expand and rise like a hen's egg would, so the results will be a little different. However, they do work to keep the ingredients together and add a little extra moisture to the recipe. To make 1 replacement egg, follow the instructions below, before adding to your recipe.

**CHIA EGG –** Stir 1 tablespoon of chia seeds with 2½ tablespoons of warm water and set aside for 5 minutes.

**FLAX EGG –** Stir 1 tablespoon of ground flax seeds with 3 tablespoons of warm water and set aside for 10–15 minutes.

**EGG REPLACERS –** In recent years, it has become much easier to purchase egg replacers in supermarkets. Look out for either powdered versions or products in the fresh fridge aisle. These are used predominantly in baking.

**EGG WASH ALTERNATIVES –** When a recipe calls for an egg wash, this is to give a little sheen to your bake, especially pastry. Use plant-based milk as a substitute (soy, almond or coconut milk works best), or aquafaba – the liquid that comes in a can of chickpeas. Or, alternatively, a little oil works very well too.

## Nut-free cooking

When a recipe calls for peanut butter or crushed nuts, there are some options you can choose, depending on your specific allergies. If possible, opt to substitute for nut-free butters like tahini, sunflower, or other specific nut-free butters, which now exist on the market. You could also leave out the nuts altogether. However, please note that nut butters may be added as a binder or for extra moisture, so the end result may differ slightly.

## Gluten-free cooking

Gluten is the name of a protein found in wheat and some other grains. If you follow a gluten-free diet, there are plenty of alternatives. In most cases, plain (all-purpose) or self-raising flour can be replaced in like-for-like quantities with shop-bought gluten-free variations. Also, look out for gluten-free baking powder, soy sauce, Worcestershire sauce, mustard and stock cubes, as some of these products may contain traces of gluten. While oats don't contain gluten, they are often processed in factories with other grains that do, so always look for oats marked as 'gluten-free' to avoid any cross contamination.

## Meat replacement in recipes

**VEGGIES –** You can generally replace meat with either firm vegetables like mushrooms or butternut squash, or meat-replacement products. Just be mindful that meat-replacement products often contain added salt, so factor this in when serving to little ones. They are also usually low in fat, therefore it is important to replace this lost fat with other forms of higher calorific foods like avocado or nut butters, especially when serving to babies, as little ones need those extra calories to help them grow.

**TOFU –** This is an excellent meat replacement. Use the correct firmness and follow the instructions on the packet to incorporate it into the recipe. Soft silken tofu is a good substitute for thick cream in desserts or to add at the end of cooking soups, while firm tofu is great to breadcrumb and turn into nuggets, or stir through pasta or noodle dishes.

Be mindful that there are hidden traces of meat and fish in some foods like Worcestershire sauce, which usually contains anchovies, so try to find vegetarian options or leave these ingredients out. Some cheeses use animal rennet in their production – however, there are plenty on the market that are vegetarian, and this will be displayed on the packet.

### A note on vanilla extract

Traditionally vanilla extract is made using alcohol, which can seem a bit daunting offering to little ones. If adding to a recipe where it will be cooked or baked, the quantity is so little that all traces of alcohol will be removed in the cooking process. These days you can buy vanilla extract which is alcohol free and this can be added to no-cook recipes or used if your dietary requirements need to avoid alcohol. Be careful to avoid using vanilla "essence" instead of extract as this is essentially fake vanilla and not ideal to serve to little ones.

Banana Chelsea Buns
(see page 94)

# Adapting recipes for your kitchen

In this book, you will find recipes using the hob, oven, slow cooker and air fryer. However if you're missing some of these pieces of equipment, don't worry as you can definitely still make the majority of these recipes.

**AIR FRYER –** Generally using an air fryer is quicker because you don't need to wait for it to heat up. This is great for use for recipes where the objective is to crisp up the food – so meats or little bakes. Anything wet and saucy isn't right for the air fryer. Ensure you keep the food spaced out in your air fryer, to allow the air to circulate and crisp up the food (the same as for oven cooking). However, for this reason, you may need to cook food in small batches for optimum results.

**SLOW COOKER –** This is great for any wet and saucy foods. If a recipe calls to cook on the hob or in the oven in a lidded pot, you can do this in the slow cooker. Ideally sear any meat beforehand, but most of the time it isn't necessary. Place all the ingredients in the slow cooker, place the lid on and the nature of the recipe will determine the time. If a recipe calls for 30 minutes hob or oven cooking, generally you'll need to allow 4–6 hours on LOW or 1½–3 hours on HIGH increasing the time accordingly. This is trial and error, but it's hard to go very wrong. Do note that you will need less liquid than if you're following an oven or hob recipe, as the evaporation rate is different. So add a little less than stated and keep an eye on it, adding more liquid if you feel it needs it.

Converting slow-cooker meals for the oven or hob is fairly easy to do. Start by searing the main element of the dish if it is a meat-based recipe. Then add the remaining ingredients, along with a little extra liquid if you feel it needs it. Cook until tender, depending on the original timings. Use your intuition here – don't worry about getting it wrong, you'll know when it's cooked, just keep checking every 10 minutes or so.

**Carrot Chips**
(see page 72)

# Batch cooking

There's two ways to approach batch cooking. One is to allot time to make up specific meals for days to come and pack them away in the fridge or freezer. Or, alternatively, my favourite method is to cook for your next meal, but make plenty so you can pack away the leftovers for later.

## Where to start?

Pick your family's favourite meals to batch cook. If you love the food, you're more likely to defrost it and enjoy those leftovers rather than letting them go to waste. If you're new to batch cooking, only make enough for one or two extra portions to avoid the feeling of eating the same thing all the time. Make a plan, shop for the extra ingredients, then allocate enough time to prep and pack up your batch-cooked meals.

## Storing batch-cooked meals

Ensure you're using the correct containers for each item – this will be listed on the recipe. If it specifies an airtight container, a glass, plastic or silicone container that seals airtight is perfect, but you can also use reusable plastic bags here as long as they can seal tight. Items that do not spoil easily like baked breaded items can be stored at room temperature, but it's best to store in an airtight container too.

If freezing, sealing items well helps to maintain the shelf life in the freezer, and minimizes freezer burn, which may spoil food too. And remember to always fully cool foods before putting them in the freezer.

Ensure you label all leftovers well, especially if they are heading for the freezer. Frozen foods can often look unrecognizable, so use a label to state what it is, and when it was frozen or the date it needs to be eaten by. You can buy fancy labels to write on, but I find a bit of cheap masking tape and a pen does the job perfectly.

For further tips on storing leftovers, turn to page 31.

## How long will meals last in the fridge?

This really depends on what the meal is. Generally 2–3 days is best to maintain flavour and texture – however, the longer you keep an item the more the taste will be compromised. For individual recipes, see the "Love your leftovers" note at the bottom of each page.

## Further tips you may find useful

Foods that overcook easily like pasta and green veggies will taste different once reheated as they will have been cooked for longer and softened more

**Carrot and Orange
Cake Cookies**
(see page 224)

in the process. This isn't a bad thing, and they still will be delicious, but it's worth remembering, so if you are intentionally batch cooking, reserve the food a little earlier when it's not quite fully cooked and use this to store away. That way once it's reheated it won't be overcooked.

Split foods into small portions, smaller than a normal single serving. This way you can defrost a couple of portions each time, and avoid having to defrost or reheat too much, which may lead to waste.

If you can, freeze foods in ovenproof dishes, like glass containers which can also go in the oven. This makes it easier to defrost and cook at the same time.

Utilize your slow cooker for batch cooking. It's easy to make a large portion in your slow cooker, perfect for storing away leftovers. You can also make up slow cooker freezer dump bags where you prepare all the ingredients for the slow cooker, place in a freezer-safe bag and freeze for a later date. Great to do a couple at a time. Then defrost overnight and, in the morning, simply add to a slow cooker. When you get home later, dinner is ready, easy peasy!

# Tips for shopping on a budget

The cost of doing a food shop seems to be going up and up, so here's some tips on how to minimize that extra spending. Before you shop or even leave the house, take an audit of what you have already in your cupboards, making a special note of what needs to be used up immediately.

Write a meal plan for however many days you will be shopping for. Incorporate those ingredients you need to use up into this plan to minimize waste.

Only buy perishables that you need – getting what you will use will help you to avoid waste.

Then write a shopping list! This has to be my number one way of saving money. Write a list and stick to it, then you won't over-shop or under-shop, saving on multiple trips to the shops that end up costing more in the long run.

However, often buying ingredients in bulk is much cheaper than smaller quantities, so, if possible, buy more, cook more and save meals for later. For more tips on batch cooking see pages 26–27.

Check your freezer regularly and rotate foods from the back to ensure these get used up within their use-by dates.

When shopping for fruits and vegetables, buying foods in season often works out cheaper. So save the strawberry recipes for summer, and apple recipes for the autumn.

Don't be tempted to shop all the deals. "10 per cent off if you buy two" may look appealing, but often it doesn't work out cheaper than if you stick to what you originally planned to buy, especially if it won't get eaten.

Basic supermarket staples are completely fine to use. They are often the cheapest but have the exact same ingredients as the more expensive alternatives. Things like canned tomatoes and beans are great value and quality, even when shopping the budget ranges in most cases.

Never shop on an empty stomach, you'll either buy too many impulse purchases, or forget things you really needed. It's an old wives' tale, but I reckon it really does work.

Sometimes shopping online stops you from being sucked into end-of-aisle promotions!

Buying fresh vegetables is fantastic, but there are some fallbacks. You often can only buy in larger packs leading to possible food waste, and you're on a short time clock until they go bad in the fridge. Therefore I'm a huge fan of using frozen vegetables. Very often they are much cheaper than the fresh produce, and they last much longer in the freezer. And an added bonus is that their nutritional value is not affected, and in some cases it's even more nutritious to buy frozen veggies over fresh as over time some fresh vegetables lose their goodness.

If you can, limit the amount of times you head out shopping. Try to do one big shop rather than many small ones, as each visit to the store is another opportunity to buy things you don't need.

# From the pantry

These are all the staple ingredients that you will see in the ingredients lists of the recipes in this book (under "From the pantry"). They are all the relatively inexpensive items I keep stocked up on, to make cooking easier and cheaper. This isn't an exhaustive list, so do add your family's favourite pantry staples here too.

| Fridge/freezer | Store cupboard/baking | Spices and cooking |
| --- | --- | --- |
| Unsalted butter | Caster sugar (golden or white) | Ground cinnamon |
| Milk | Vanilla extract | Cooking flavourless oil like sunflower or vegetable oil (garlic infused olive oil too if you wish) |
| A selection of frozen veg | Regular porridge oats | |
| A selection of frozen fruit | Flour (self-raising and plain) | Garlic granules |
| | Baking powder | Black pepper, ideally freshly ground |
| | Bread flour | |
| | Honey | Smoked paprika |
| | Sesame seeds | Low-salt soy sauce |
| *Storing baked goods* | Eggs (medium) | Sesame oil |
| Biscuits and crackers can be stored at room temperature. Keep in airtight containers in a cool, dry environment. | Cornflour | Low-salt stock cubes (chicken, beef or vegetable) |
| | Soft brown sugar | |
| | Dried pasta | Mixed dried herbs |
| | Rice | Tomato purée |
| | Passata | Mild curry powder |
| | Cans of chopped tomatoes | Whole garlic bulbs |
| | Canned sweetcorn | Worcestershire sauce |
| | Cans of beans (butter, red kidney) and chickpeas | Ground cumin |
| | | Dried thyme |

- Eggs in their shell, as the shell may crack once frozen due to the water content. This is a health risk.

- Fresh veg that has a high water content like celery, lettuce and cucumber. They will freeze with ice crystals which melt during thawing, leaving you with soggy veg.

- Food emulsions, such as mayonnaise, will separate and curdle once defrosted.

- Soft cheese and dairy like yogurt with a high water content will also separate once defrosted. This is safe to eat – however, the consistency will be different.

**Safety guide for heating leftovers**

- Leftovers should only ever be reheated once.

- Never freeze meat or fish twice.

- You can defrost fruit and veg, cook with them, then freeze that cooked meal.

- Always use airtight containers for storing leftovers.

# Storage and freezing guidelines

Storing and freezing food safely is important, especially when feeding little tummies. It really comes down to how and when you package up the food to determine when and for how long you can store it. For specific instructions for each recipe within this book, look out for the "Love your leftovers" section of each recipe.

## How to store food in the fridge

- Ensure you always put leftover food in airtight containers when storing in the fridge. This not only slows down the growth of bacteria, but helps to stop other food flavours leaching into all the food in your fridge.

- Always fully cool food before putting it in the fridge. Putting hot or warm food in the fridge adjusts the temperature of your fridge and therefore compromises the other food you are storing.

- Try to cool food as quickly as possible by spreading evenly on a cool surface before storing in the fridge. Ideally cool within 2 hours – however, if you are storing rice, ensure it is fully cooled and refrigerated within 1 hour of cooking.

- A general rule of thumb is that most leftover cooked food will last for 2 days in the fridge. However, some more perishable foods will only last for 24 hours, for example, cooked fish.

- Always store raw meat on a separate shelf from fresh fruit and veg.

## How to store food in the freezer

- Ensure you package up all foods in airtight containers or bags to prevent freezer burn.

- Try to freeze in portions so you only need to defrost what you need. If freezing individual foods like fritters, these can stick together in the freezer. To prevent this, place a small square of non-stick baking paper in between each item to stop them sticking together.

- Label and date the food you put in the freezer so you can ensure you aren't keeping it for longer than is safe.

- Always store frozen raw meat on a different shelf to frozen fruit and veg, as this may be eaten uncooked.

## Reheating leftover chilled food

Some food can be eaten cold after storing in the fridge or defrosting, as long as it was fully cooked beforehand. Fruit like berries can be eaten uncooked after defrosting, and fritters can be eaten cold from the fridge or once defrosted. However, if you choose to reheat the food, you must ensure the food is completely piping hot before cooling and serving. It can be tempting to heat just a little, especially if serving to little ones – however, this is dangerous as bacteria risk increases at this temperature.

Keeping food cold under 8°C means the bacteria is at dormant level, and is safe to consume, or heat food to over 70°C "piping hot", to kill off the bacteria in the food. You can then cool the food to a safe warm temperature to feed to your little one. Don't forget to ensure your fridge is always at 5°C or less to ensure food is stored at a safe temperature too.

## Reheating frozen food

Generally the best advice is to fully defrost food in the fridge before reheating and serving. However, some food can be cooked straight from frozen, which vastly saves on time.

If you defrost food at room temperature, keep an eye on when it is defrosted and place it in the fridge straight away – storing defrosted food at room temperature for prolonged periods of time can compromise the safety of that food.

Foods that are raw inside need to be defrosted first, as when cooking the outside will cook and burn before the inside has had a chance to do so. However, foods like fritters can be reheated in the microwave from frozen until piping hot as this will not compromise on the texture and flavour.

To defrost 3 pancakes (see page 42) stack in the microwave, place on a non-metal plate and blast on full power for 60 seconds. Remove, separate and flip, then place on the plate flat with the coldest side up, then put back in the microwave in 30 second blasts, checking between each, until piping hot.

Foods like cooked and frozen Garlic Mushroom Twists (see page 80) can be placed on a baking tray from frozen and baked in an oven at 180°C fan (200°C/400°F/Gas 6) for 5–10 minutes until piping hot inside. The exact time is dependent on size, however, it's important you keep an eye on foods like this, as there is a fine line between perfectly done and burnt.

# How to repurpose leftovers

Unused and uneaten leftover cooked meals are one of the biggest contributors to food waste. It's very easy to cook too much food, to store it with the best intentions to eat it another day, but for whatever reason that does not happen.

Often it can be down to a lack of desire to eat the same kind of food again. So, my favourite way to enjoy leftovers is to turn them into another meal with a whole new texture and flavour profile.

There is no hard and fast rule on how to do this, as it really depends on what you've got to start with, but here are a few of my favourite transformations:

**Leftover soup –** I always seem to be left with a small amount of soup and it's fantastic made into a pasta sauce the next day. Add the soup to a wide frying pan and simmer until some of the moisture has evaporated, this depends on how thick the soup was to start with. You can stir through some thick cream cheese to help it thicken, or add a cornflour slurry (1 tablespoon of cornflour [cornstarch] mixed with 2 tablespoons of cold water) which will help it thicken more. Remove from the heat, add a handful of grated hard cheese and toss through freshly cooked pasta.

**Leftover pasta –** My favourite way to enjoy leftover pasta is to make it into a pasta bake the next day. Before you store your leftovers, pour the still warm pasta into an ovenproof dish, allow to cool in this, then cover and refrigerate. Then when you're ready for the next meal, add a splash of water or milk to the now hard pasta, this will help add back more moisture, then top with grated cheese and bake for 15–20 minutes in a hot oven until crisp on top and piping hot throughout.

**Leftover pasta bake –** If you've made a pasta bake to begin with, for example baked macaroni cheese, once cool this can be quite firm. I love to chop it into squares, dip in a little flour, then some beaten egg, followed by any breadcrumbs you have in. Then either fry quickly for a few minutes on each side, or bake at 200°C fan (220°C/425°F/Gas 7) or air-fry at 200°C (400°F) for 15–20 minutes until crisp on the outside and soft inside. Utterly delicious. This works well for a firm set lasagne and leftover risotto too.

**Leftover roast meat –** For chicken, the meat can be used to make sandwiches, quesadillas (check out page 110), omelettes or quick pasta dishes. It's great to make a lasagne or chicken pie. The meat-removed bones are fantastic boiled in a big pot of water with an onion and some chunky carrots. Thirty minutes will do, then strain and add some broccoli, cook until tender, then blend for a delicious soup.

For pork, lamb and beef – I like to chop leftovers into chunks, then add to a frying pan with 1 teaspoon each of smoked paprika, cumin, mixed herbs and a generous grinding of black pepper and fry in a little oil until crisp. Delicious with flatbreads or pitta and a yogurt dip.

Leftover Roast Crispy
**Quesadillas**
(see pages 110–111)

# Tips for reducing food waste

**Fruit bowl roulette** Do you find fruit in your fruit bowl is often going off before you have a chance to eat it? It might be worth storing those bananas elsewhere, as bananas release a gas called ethene which speeds up the ripening of other fruits. Equally, if you have a hard piece of fruit you wish to ripen quicker, put a few bananas on top and it'll help you along.

**Get herby!** Don't let your garlic and herbs go to waste. Chop them up fine and add to a freezer bag to use on their own, adding to any recipe you please. Or you can add them to a little bit of oil to make a flavourful accompaniment to any meal. Unsterilized containers of simple olive oil and herbs mixed together will last in the fridge for up to 2 weeks.

**Are you cool enough?** Check whether your fridge is cool enough, just a few degrees too warm could mean your milk is turning sour quicker or your veggies are softening faster. It should be between 0–5°C.

**Chill your bread** In the UK, we don't often store our bread in the fridge, let alone in the freezer, but it can help to maximize its shelf life. Perfect for loaves you plan to toast anyway! If you're not keen on this idea, you can chop stale leftover bread into small croutons, bake in a low oven until completely dried out, then pulse in a food processor to your desired consistency. These breadcrumbs will store in an airtight container for 2 months in a cool, dark place, or freeze for up to 6 months.

**Don't be afraid to switch things up** If you could only get a larger amount of food than you expected, try to incorporate this into your meal plan to avoid leftovers going to waste.

**Freeze those scraps!** Instead of throwing away vegetable and potato peelings, ensure the veg is clean before peeling, then store those scraps in a bag in the freezer. Keep adding to the bag whenever you have some scraps, then when the bag is full you can make a delicious soup, or blend up and add to stews for an extra veggie hit.

**Stick to the plan!** Shop according to your meal plan and shopping list.

**Seal it up!** Food lasts much longer in the fridge when it is stored in an airtight container. So box up those berries and keep the open packet of ham in a sealable bag, as this will prevent foods from dehydrating too quickly and spoiling.

# Meal plans

Here's a couple of examples of weekly meal plans with ideas on what to do
with any leftovers, using recipes within this book. Not every day needs to
be filled with freshly cooked items – leftovers are delicious and a great way
to make the pennies stretch further.

## Chicken Cheese Melt

Leftover chicken meatballs are delicious reheated on their own, or make
them into this scrummy grilled cheese sandwich.

First, reheat the meatballs by placing your desired amount into a
microwaveable bowl and adding a decent splash of water. Not too much to
drown the meat, but enough to see a small pool at the bottom of the bowl.
Now add a small knob of butter, along with extra seasoning if you wish.
Cover tightly and microwave for 3½ minutes on HIGH, tossing the chicken
meatballs halfway through to ensure they reheat thoroughly. You can also
use the same method in a pan and heat for 6–10 minutes until bubbling
and the balls are piping hot throughout.

Now, to make your sarnies, take a thick slice of bread and lightly toast to
firm up the texture. Now spread over a layer of cream cheese and halve or
slice the chicken meatballs to layer on top. Cover with cheese, grated firm
mozzarella or Cheddar work best, but any of your favourite firm cheeses
will be good. Place under a hot grill and heat until the cheese has melted
and turned golden. Delicious with a salad and some pickles on the side.

| Day | Breakfast | Lunch | Dinner |
|---|---|---|---|
| Sunday | Carrot Banana Pancakes (page 42) | Sunday Dinner Pork Belly (page 208) | Cheese and Onion Bakes (page 70) |
| Monday | PB & J No-cook Porridge (page 44) | Cinnamon and Raisin Loaf (page 58) | Sesame Mushroom Chinese Pork (using finely chopped leftover pork instead of mince, page 116) |
| Tuesday | Leftover Cinnamon and Raisin Loaf and fresh fruit | Courgette and Chicken Meatballs (page 144) | Garlic Teriyaki Chicken Noodles (page 190) |
| Wednesday | Leftover Cinnamon and Raisin Loaf toasted and topped with mashed raspberries | Chicken Cheese Melt (see left for recipe) | Glamorgan Sausages (pages 171–172) |
| Thursday | Savoury Sesame Oats (page 46) | Crispy Paprika Fish (page 78) and salad | Fajita Lasagne (pages 135–136) |
| Friday | Emperor's Crumbs (page 54) | Leftover Fajita Lasagne with salad | Rebecca's Sloppy Joes (page 112) |
| Saturday | Fridge Raid Vegetable Egg Loaf (page 64) | Garlic Mushroom Twists (page 80) | Leftover Sloppy Joes Pasta (page 114) |

# Meat-free meal plan

### Leftover Sunday Roast Frittata

If you have some leftover lentil and squash roast, it makes a delicious frittata. Firstly, chop it into small chunks, along with any leftover roast potatoes too, which work so well here.

To a very large frying pan, add the chopped leftovers along with a little drizzle of sunflower oil. Stir and toss to cook over a medium-high heat. You want the edges to crisp up and turn golden, plus heating up throughout. Once crisp, you can add any leftover cooked veg you may have too, chopped up into chunks as well.

Once thoroughly heated through, add in 6 whisked eggs and allow the egg to cook and set at the bottom for a few minutes. Sprinkle over some cheese, then place under the grill for 3–5 minutes until the egg has set and the cheese melted.

This can also be cooked in a large dish in the air fryer, similar to the Savoury Cheesecake Egg Cups on page 76.

| Day | Breakfast | Lunch | Dinner |
|-----|-----------|-------|--------|
| Sunday | Strawberry Breakfast Muffins (page 66) | Cauli and Broccoli Cheese Soup with Garlic Toast (page 181) | Lentil Butternut Squash Roast (page 166) with roast potatoes |
| Monday | Leftover Strawberry Breakfast Muffins | Leftover Sunday Roast Frittata (see recipe left) | Baked Coconut Lentil Rice (page 158) with veggies |
| Tuesday | Cereal Breakfast Bars (page 60) | Crispy Korean Green Bean Pancakes (page 164) | Frugal Mushroom Lasagne (pages 169–170) |
| Wednesday | Banana Bread Porridge Loaf (page 52) | Leftover Frugal Mushroom Lasagne with salad | Leek and Potato Soup (page 198) with Korean Garlic Bread (page 178) |
| Thursday | Leftover Banana Bread Porridge Loaf | Curried Rösti Pasties (page 160) | Butter Bean Pasta with Garlic Crunchy Sesame Crumbs (page 176) |
| Friday | Freezer stash Cereal Bars | Leftover Butter Bean Pasta | Sunshine Veg Tart (page 162) |
| Saturday | Gnarly Smoky Bean Taquitos (page 51) | Leftover Sunshine Veg Tart with salad | Tofu, Sesame and Soy Noodles (page 182) |

# Breakfast

# Carrot Banana Pancakes

Spiced fluffy pancakes with some hidden fruit and veg in there too. It always feels like such a win when you start the day with a portion of veggies, and these pancakes make it so easy to do so.

GF*
EF*
DF*
V
Vg*

Makes 12 pancakes

Prep 5 mins, Cook 10 mins

## Ingredients

1 large carrot, approx. 100g (3½oz)

1 ripe banana

### From the pantry

2 eggs*

60ml (¼ cup) milk*

120g (scant 1 cup) self-raising flour*

2 tsp ground cinnamon

sunflower oil

Wash the carrot, trim off the woody ends and finely grate on the smallest setting of a box grater. There's no need to peel, there's lots of nutrients in the skin, and it also saves time too.

Add the grated carrot to a bowl, along with the banana. With the back of a fork, mash the banana into the carrot to form a purée.

Now add the eggs and milk and whisk to combine. Measure in the flour and cinnamon and stir briefly until smooth.

Preheat a large non-stick pan over a medium heat and, once the pan is hot, drizzle a tiny amount of oil into the pan. Take a tablespoon and add spoonful amounts of the batter into the pan, spreading into small circles. Depending on the size of your pan, do this in batches of approx. 5 pancakes.

Turn the heat to low and cook for 2 minutes or so until you start to see small bubbles forming on the top of the pancakes. Take a thin, sturdy plastic spatula and flip each pancake quickly and confidently to cook the other side for a further couple of minutes. It's better to cook these pancakes over a lower heat to avoid the outside burning and the inside staying raw, as cooking over a low heat ensures they cook through evenly.

Once all done, transfer to a plate and repeat with the remaining batter. Serve with a little natural yogurt, crushed nuts if you have some, and a drizzle of honey for everyone older than 12 months. If serving to babies, cut each pancake into fine strips so it's easier for them to hold.

### Love your leftovers

Leftovers will keep for 2 days in an airtight container at room temperature, or freeze with non-stick baking paper between each pancake, for up to 3 months. To defrost, place in the toaster until completely defrosted and piping hot throughout.

For extra sweetness, add in a small handful of seedless raisins. If they're large, chop before adding if you're serving to little ones.

# PB & J No-cook Porridge

Peanut butter and jelly (jam to us British folk), a classic flavour combo, made into a delicious easy no-cook cold porridge. It's great for prep ahead meals, or breakfast on the go, or just when you fancy avoiding using the hob on busy mornings.

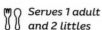

**Serves 1 adult and 2 littles**

**Prep 5 mins, Rest 15 mins**

## Ingredients

approx. 130g (4½oz) frozen or fresh raspberries

140ml (scant ⅔ cup) milk*

100g (½ cup) Greek-style yogurt*

1 heaped tbsp (smooth or crunchy) peanut butter (approx. 35g/1oz)

### From the pantry

100g (1 cup) rolled porridge oats*

1 tbsp honey, maple syrup or sugar (optional)*

---

If using frozen raspberries, measure out now and set aside to begin defrosting.

In a bowl, add the oats, milk, yogurt and honey, maple syrup or sugar, if using. Mix all together very well, then dollop in the peanut butter and add the raspberries. Stir well, the raspberries will start to break up and turn everything a lovely hue of pink. Try to leave some raspberries a little chunkier, this gives the jam effect when eating.

Cover and set aside for 15 minutes, or refrigerate overnight. I like to spoon into the kids' serving bowls first so it's even easier in the morning.

Serve as is, or with a little dollop of extra yogurt on top. You could also raid your cupboards for extra toppings, add a sprinkling of desiccated coconut, some chocolate chips, a little more sweetness on top if us adults prefer, and to ramp up the fruit intake, add some extra chopped fruit on top.

The finished dish will have a deliciously rich and comforting thick texture which is what makes this breakfast so moreish, but if you would prefer, serve with a little extra milk to thin down the consistency. You can also heat up for serving, 2 minutes on HIGH in the microwave or a couple of minutes stirring constantly in a saucepan. Add some extra milk to avoid the mixture sticking to the pan.

### ♡ Love your leftovers

Leftovers will keep for 3 days covered in the fridge, or you can freeze in portions for up to 2 months. Allow to defrost thoroughly before serving or defrost and reheat until piping hot with a little extra milk in a saucepan or microwave, stirring often and heating in bursts.

Opt for the cheap and cheerful flattened porridge oats rather than the thicker whole-looking oats, as these take longer for the liquid to soak in.

# Savoury Sesame Oats

Loosely based on the Chinese breakfast staple, congee, this savoury porridge is a delicious variation on the sweet version. Plus there's some extra veggies in there too.

 **Serves 2 adults and 2 littles**

 **Prep and cook 10 mins**

## Ingredients

1 medium courgette, approx. 200g (7oz)

250ml (generous 1 cup) milk*

70g (2½oz) Cheddar cheese, grated*

### From the pantry

flavourless oil or a knob of butter, for frying*

1 tbsp low-salt soy sauce

1 tsp sesame oil

1 tsp garlic granules or purée

130g (1⅓ cups) rolled porridge oats*

½ low-salt chicken or vegetable stock cube* (optional)

4 eggs

freshly ground black pepper

sesame seeds, to serve

Coarsely grate the courgette (peel first if you prefer to hide the veggies), then add to a medium non-stick saucepan over a medium-high heat. Sauté for 3–4 minutes until softened, add a little flavourless oil or a knob of butter if you find it is sticking.

Meanwhile, measure the milk into a jug and add 250ml (generous 1 cup) of water to the milk. Add the soy sauce, sesame oil and garlic and stir well.

Once the courgette has softened, add the porridge oats, followed by all of the liquid. Crumble in the half stock cube, add a grinding of black pepper, then stir everything really well. I like to use a rubber spatula here to help stop the oats from sticking to the pan. Stir and cook for 3–5 minutes until the oats have plumped up and softened and all the liquid has been absorbed.

While the oats cook, fry your eggs. Heat a large non-stick pan, drizzle with a little oil and, once hot, crack in the eggs and fry to your preferred doneness.

Once the oats are cooked, remove the pan from the heat, add the cheese and stir for 15 seconds to melt. Now it's ready to serve. Give everyone a dollop of porridge, followed by a fried egg on top, and lastly a sprinkling of sesame seeds. Add a touch of sesame oil too if you would like to amplify the flavour. Adults, you can add a little extra soy sauce to your portion along with a little extra pepper and try it with some chilli oil for a kick to start your day.

 ## Love your leftovers

The porridge will last, covered, in the fridge for 2 days or freeze in portions for up to 3 months. Defrost thoroughly and reheat in a saucepan or microwave with an extra splash of milk or water to loosen the consistency.

Delicious with a runny or a hard-boiled egg on top. Babies from 6 months old can have runny yolks as long as the eggs are British Lion stamped. See note on page 12.

Gnarly Smoky Bean Taquitos (see page 51)

# Breakfast Taquitos

We have plain cheesy taquitos which are delicious in their own right, or how about trying tomato and herb, or my gnarly smoky bean taquitos too?

V

**Makes 2-3 small taquitos**

**Prep and cook 10 mins**

## Ingredients

approx. 40g (1½oz) Cheddar cheese, grated*

2 mini tortilla wraps*

............

**From the pantry**

1 heaped tsp unsalted butter*

2 eggs

**Love your leftovers**

All three variations will store in the fridge for up to 2 days in an airtight container. You can also freeze by wrapping individually and freezing for up to 3 months. Defrost thoroughly, then reheat in the oven at 180°C fan (200°C/400°F/ Gas 6) for 5–10 minutes until piping hot throughout. Or pan-fry over a low heat until the outside is crisp again and the inside piping hot.

## Simple Cheesy Egg Taquito

Add the butter to a large non-stick frying pan, over a medium-high heat. While it's melting, crack the eggs into a small bowl and quickly whisk with a fork until the yolks and whites are completely incorporated.

Once the butter has melted, grab a silicone spatula, which creates a tight seal when scraping inside bowls, and use this to get every last drop of egg into the frying pan. We want to scramble the eggs now, so gently move the cooked firmer egg around using the spatula, scraping the egg away from the bottom of the pan and the sides, ensuring that as you move the cooked egg, the uncooked egg can run down and touch the hot pan. You want to move the eggs just enough to ensure it all cooks, but try to avoid vigorously stirring, as this breaks up the egg and will result in lots of small pieces. This should only take 1–2 minutes, so don't leave it, as it'll most likely overcook.

When the eggs are still wet and not completely cooked, add half the cheese, fold and take the pan off the heat.

Lay the tortilla wraps on a board, and add half of the eggs to each tortilla, in a line down the centre. Then roll them up as tightly as you can without the filling spilling out and place back in the pan, seam-side down to seal it first. Place the pan over a high heat again, and sprinkle the remaining cheese over each tortilla. Don't worry if some falls onto the pan, this will stick to the other side as you flip it over. After 1–2 minutes, the underneath should have turned a little golden, and your cheese melted. Use a spatula to flip the taquitos over, and cook on the other side for another 1–2 minutes until the cheese has turned a little crispy.

Serve with fruit and yogurt for dipping for breakfast, or with a little salad for lunch. Adults, these are particularly good with hot sauce too.

## Ingredients

390g (13¾oz) cannellini beans in water

60g (2¼oz) Cheddar cheese, grated*

4 mini tortilla wraps*

...............

### From the pantry

2 tbsp tomato purée (paste)

2 heaped tsp smoked paprika

1 tsp garlic granules

a little oil, for frying

## Gnarly Smoky Bean Taquitos

To a large non-stick frying pan, add the tomato purée and, using a spoon, add the beans straight out of the can, leaving most of the water in the can but allowing approximately 2 tablespoons to go into the pan for added moisture. No need to measure this, but retain the water in the can, if needed later.

Mix the tomato purée into the beans and allow to come up to temperature and simmer. Meanwhile, add the smoked paprika and garlic granules and stir well. If it all seems too dry, then add a small dash of the bean water to loosen it all up, but be careful not to add too much, as it'll make the sauce too runny.

Once the beans are piping hot, remove the pan from the heat and stir in half of the cheese before transferring the beans to a small bowl if you only intend to make a small amount of taquitos now. If you're going to make them all now, lay the tortillas on a chopping board and divide the mixture between the four. Take a piece of kitchen paper and briefly wipe down the pan, no need for it to be completely clean, but do remove most of the sauce as it'll burn at the next stage.

Place the pan back over a high heat and add a drizzle of oil. Once hot, roll up the taquitos, and place in the pan, seam-side down. Sprinkle over the remaining cheese and cook on each side for 1–2 minutes until gnarly and crisp.

## Ingredients

1 large or 2 smaller salad tomatoes

approx. 20g (¾oz) Cheddar cheese, grated*

3 mini tortilla wraps*

...............

### From the pantry

1 tsp sunflower or garlic oil

2 eggs, whisked

¼ tsp mixed dried herbs

freshly ground black pepper

## Tomato and Herb Taquitos

Dice the tomatoes as small as you can, then add to a cold frying pan with your oil of choice. While they come up to temperature, add the eggs to a small bowl along with a little black pepper and the dried herbs, then whisk well. Once there's lots of heat in the pan and the tomatoes are starting to sizzle, add the eggs and scramble as above until you see no wet runny eggs or tomato liquid.

If serving to little ones under 2, mash their beans with the back of a fork before rolling up in their wrap, as larger beans can pose a choking hazard.

# Banana Bread Porridge Loaf

Don't be put off by the number of ingredients here, they're all super cheap and most you probably already have in. A slice of this breakfast loaf is the perfect well-balanced brekkie for all the fam. Add some 100% nut butter on top to get in those essential fatty acids and nutrients.

**GF\***

**DF\***

**V**

**Vg\***

 **Makes 1 medium loaf**

**Prep 10 mins, Bake 40-45 mins**

## Ingredients

2 large, ripe bananas

100g (scant ½ cup) unsalted butter* or sunflower oil, plus extra for greasing

100g (3½oz) raisins or sultanas

### From the pantry

3 eggs

30g (2 tbsp) caster sugar (superfine) (optional)

2 tsp vanilla extract

150g (1½ cups) porridge oats*

2 tsp ground cinnamon

200g (1½ cups) self-raising flour*

1 tsp baking powder*

Preheat the oven to 170°C fan (190°C/375°F/Gas 5). Line a 900g (2lb) loaf tin with non-stick baking paper and grease any sides that are still exposed.

In a large mixing bowl, add the bananas and mash with the back of a fork. Crack in the eggs and add the melted butter or oil, along with the sugar, if using, and vanilla extract. Whisk well to combine.

If your dried fruits are quite large, run a knife over them to cut into smaller sizes, then add to the banana mixture along with the oats and cinnamon, stirring to combine. Sift the flour and baking powder into the batter and briefly mix together until you see no white flour but be sure to avoid overmixing as this will prevent your loaf from being light.

Pour the batter into your prepared loaf tin, level out the top and scatter a few oats over the top before placing on the middle shelf of your oven to bake for 40–45 minutes until well risen and an inserted knife comes out clean.

Allow to sit for 5 minutes before lifting out of the tin and placing on a cooling rack to go cold to slice. You can enjoy warm but note that if you cut into it when it's still very warm you run the risk of the bread drying out sooner than it normally would.

This bread is great on its own, with a little butter, honey or jam for children over one. And as it gets staler, refresh in the toaster for a crispy on the outside and soft in the middle texture. So yum!

### ♡ Love your leftovers

Leftovers will keep in an airtight container at room temperature for up to a week or freeze in slices for up to 3 months. Defrost in the toaster until piping hot throughout.

# Emperor's Crumbs

Growing up with a Hungarian mother in the north of England, she would often make us traditional dishes like this one. Translated as Császármorzsa in Hungarian, it reminds me of my childhood, like a big cosy hug in a bowl when eating it. We used to always have this as a pudding, but as my version is lower in sugar it's perfect to have for breakfast on slower weekend mornings.

 **Serves 2 adults and 2 littles**

 **Prep 5 mins, Cook 7-10 mins**

## Ingredients

250g (9oz) fine semolina

1 x 400g (14oz) can of apricots in juice, to serve

### From the pantry

175ml (¾ cup) milk*

3 eggs

2 tsp vanilla extract

2 tbsp flavourless oil like sunflower

To a bowl, add the semolina, crack in the eggs, add the vanilla extract and half of the milk. Start to stir with a whisk, then gradually add the remaining milk. Whisk until you have a smooth thick batter, a little like a thick stack pancake batter consistency.

Now this bit will feel strange but trust the process. Take a large non-stick frying pan and add the oil. Set over a medium-high heat and allow the oil to warm up. Then pour all the batter into the pan, scraping out as much as you can from the bowl. Take a wooden or plastic spatula, sturdy and flat-ended, and begin to move the batter around, scraping up what is touching the bottom of the pan – a little like as if you're making scrambled eggs. Very soon the mixture will start to become very thick and clump together. Now you need to break up these large clumps into smaller chunks using the flat end of the spatula. Keep doing this, using a cutting and stirring motion, and gradually the batter will dry out and start to brown on the edges. Keep cutting the bigger chunks with your spatula until you have lots of little chunks, then allow the crumbs to sit for 1 minute to brown, stir and toss, then cook again for a few more minutes until there's lots of nice browned edges.

Portion up the Emperor's crumbs into serving bowls. Traditionally you always eat this with apricot jam and powdered sugar on top, which is utterly delicious. However, to keep the sugar content down, it's just as yummy with a few canned apricots on top and a little of the juice drizzled over the crumbs. You can add a touch of icing sugar on this too if you would prefer a sweeter taste.

 **Love your leftovers**

If you have leftovers, they will keep in the fridge for 2–3 days, enjoy cold or reheat in a frying pan until piping hot. It's great as a granola alternative with a little yogurt and fruit on the side. You can also freeze this for another day for up to 3 months. Defrost thoroughly and reheat in a frying pan.

# Savoury Emperor's Crumbs

This version of Emperor's crumbs is savoury, rather than the traditional sweet, and made with cheese and smoked paprika, with a little corn to add in some extra veggies.

 **Serves 2 adults and 2 littles**

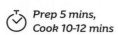 **Prep 5 mins, Cook 10-12 mins**

## Ingredients

250g (9oz) fine semolina

100g (3½oz) Cheddar cheese*, grated

### From the pantry

175ml (¾ cup) milk*

3 eggs

2 tbsp flavourless oil like sunflower

1 heaped tsp smoked paprika

freshly ground black pepper

165g (generous 1 cup) drained canned sweetcorn in water

Make the Emperor's crumbs as described on page 54, leaving out the vanilla extract this time.

Once the crumbs are starting to brown, sprinkle over the smoked paprika and add a grinding of black pepper. Give it a good stir to coat all the crumbs in the paprika.

Add the drained corn, and sprinkle over the grated cheese, reserving some for serving, then cook for a further couple of minutes, stirring often until the cheese has melted and is starting to char in parts and the corn is heated throughout.

Serve as is with a little yogurt, the reserved grated cheese and sliced avocado if you have it on the side. Adults add some salt to your portion, this is particularly delicious with some vinegary hot sauce drizzled over on top.

 **Love your leftovers**

Leftovers will keep in the fridge for 2 days to enjoy hot or cold, or freeze for 3 months. Defrost thoroughly, then add to a large frying pan to reheat over a high heat for 5 minutes until piping hot throughout.

# Cinnamon and Raisin Loaf

Fruit loaves are my Nina's favourite from the shop, but they are usually really high in added sugar. This version is much healthier, and once you buy the ingredients you can make many loaves saving a few pennies too.

**Makes 1 large loaf**

**Prep 10 mins, plus resting, Bake 30-40 mins**

## Ingredients

50g (scant ¼ cup) unsalted butter*, softened, plus (optional) extra, melted, for greasing

7g (⅙oz) dried fast action yeast

250g (1½ cups) seedless raisins

### From the pantry

500g (3¾ cups) white strong bread flour, plus extra for dusting

3 heaped tsp ground cinnamon

**Love your leftovers**

This loaf will keep in an airtight bag for 3–4 days, but just like a standard bread loaf, as the days pass it will get staler, so I opt for toasting my slices from day 3.

I find it easiest to use my stand mixer for this first stage, making this process very quick and easy. To the stand mixer bowl, add all the ingredients and 350ml (1½ cups) warm (body temperature) water.

Then, using the dough hook attachment, starting on the slow setting, start to combine all the ingredients. Once a dough is formed, turn the speed up to high and knead for 3–4 minutes until the dough comes away from the sides and the bowl is clean. Alternatively, you can knead by hand on a floured surface for approx. 10 minutes, it will feel sticky initially but keep working it and it'll come together.

Scrape the dough from the hook, press into a ball in the bowl, cover the bowl with cling film, followed by a tea towel and set aside in a warm, non draughty part of your home. Allow the dough to at least double in size, triple is ideal. Sometimes I do this the night before and place the bowl in the fridge, the warmer the environment the quicker it will rise. At standard home temperature it will take around 2 hours.

Once the dough has risen, dust your work surface with flour, then scrape the dough out. Press the dough to knock out the air (I like to form a rectangle shape as I do this). Tightly roll it up into a sausage shape and tuck the ends together so that the loaf is the same size as a 900g (2lb) loaf tin. Either sprinkle some flour into the tin, or grease with spray or melted butter to ensure the loaf will release easily. Place the bread in the tin, seam-side down. Put the tea towel back over the tin and set aside for at least 40 minutes until the bread has risen up to almost double its size again, or is rising up over the top of the tin. Preheat the oven to 160°C fan (180°C/350°F/Gas 4).

Carefully place the loaf in the centre of the oven, being careful not to bash the tin, which would knock out some of the air. Bake for 30–40 minutes until well risen and golden on top. Once you feel it's done, remove from the oven and give it a tap with your fingers, if it sounds hollow it should be baked inside. Cool fully before slicing, and serve with butter or simply on its own, delicious.

# Cereal Breakfast Bars

EF

DF*

V

Vg*

I don't know about you, but I always have loads of half empty cereal boxes in my cupboard, so this is a great way to use some of those up. Lovely and soft once baked, perfect for little taste testers.

**Makes 10 bars**

**Prep 10 mins,
Bake 20-22 mins**

## Ingredients

150g (5½oz) wheat biscuits cereal

100g (3½oz) cornflakes

1 x 415g (14½oz) can of fruit cocktail in juice

100g (scant ½ cup) peanut butter

140g (1¾ cups) seedless raisins

70g (2½oz) white chocolate*, to drizzle (optional)

Line a 23cm (9in) square baking tray with non-stick baking paper and preheat the oven to 180°C fan (200°C/400°F/Gas 6).

Add the cereal to a food processor and whizz for a few seconds to break it up. Transfer this cereal crumb to a large mixing bowl, then add just the juice from the fruit cocktail can to the blender pot, reserving the fruit for later. Add the peanut butter and raisins to the blender too, then whizz for 2–3 minutes until fully combined and the raisins have broken down a little.

Pour this mixture into the mixing bowl along with the fruit cocktail and mix it all up very well. Tip the mixture into the prepared baking tray and press down with the back of a spoon to level out the top and compress the mixture, ensuring the edges aren't sticking up too as these will catch easily.

Bake for 20–22 minutes until the top is golden and the bake has set. Allow to cool fully in the tin before lifting out using the baking paper and cutting into 10 bars. Feel free to melt the chocolate and add a drizzle to some of the bars for an extra little bit of sweetness if you wish.

 **Love your leftovers**

These will store in an airtight container at room temperature for 3–4 days, perfect for breakfast for the next few days. You can also freeze leftovers individually wrapped in baking paper, allow to thaw at room temperature and enjoy within a day.

# Peach and Apple Oat Danish

These dairy-free pastries are so sweet to whip up with the kids and feel like such a treat.

 GF*

 EF*

 DF*

 V

 Vg*

 **Makes 6**

 **Prep 10 mins, Bake 18-22 mins**

### Ingredients

250g (9oz) can peach halves or slices in juice

1 red eating apple

320g (11oz) sheet of ready-rolled puff pastry*

### From the pantry

1 tsp vanilla extract

15g (1 tbsp) caster sugar (superfine) (optional)

30g (⅓ cup) porridge oats*

1 egg, beaten, or milk*, for brushing (optional)

### ♡ Love your leftovers

Leftovers will keep in an airtight container for 4 days. I like to pop these in the air fryer at 180°C (350°F) for 5 minutes to reheat or you can enjoy cold. They will freeze well for up to 2 months. Defrost in the oven at 180°C fan (200°C/400°F/Gas 6) for 8–10 minutes until hot.

Preheat the oven to 200°C fan (220°C/425°F/Gas 7) and line a large baking sheet with non-stick baking paper.

Drain the juice from the peaches but ensure you keep the juice for later. Take out roughly 100g (3½oz) of the peaches and set aside, then add the remaining peaches to a medium flat-bottomed bowl. Using a potato masher, mash the fruit to a lumpy purée. Some larger chunks are totally fine.

Now add the vanilla, sugar, if using, and oats. Use a fine-bladed grater, like a citrus zester, and grate the apple, including the skin, down to the core and discard this. Grate over the bowl so all the pulp and juices go into the mixture and don't get lost. Now give it all a stir and set aside.

Unroll the puff pastry and cut into 6 squares, placing them on the baking sheet at least 2cm (¾in) apart. Divide the oat mix between the 6 pastry sheets, adding a mound in the middle, trying to keep the edges clean. It will feel like the mix is a little too runny but don't worry, as the oats will soak up the excess moisture as they bake.

Now take the remaining peaches, you want 2 or 3 slices for each pastry top, so slice some in half if needed. Arrange the peaches in the centre of each pastry, then dab some of the reserved fruit juice, or a little beaten egg on the exposed pastry edges. Bake for 18–22 minutes until the pastry has turned golden and puffed up.

To add an extra sheen and gloriousness to these Danishes, I urge you to do this additional step while the pastries bake, but it is completely optional. Pour the remaining juice that you saved from your can of peaches into a small saucepan. Boil it over a high heat for 5 minutes, stirring often until it has turned very thick and is almost starting to catch. The liquid will evaporate and you'll be left with a fruit syrup which is glossy and sweet.

When the pastries are done, straight away brush all over the fruit and pastry with this fruity syrup. Now enjoy with a little extra fruit on the side. For little ones, serve in finger strips with a little Greek yogurt for dunking.

# Fridge Raid Vegetable Egg Loaf

GF*

DF*

V

This is a great one for using up leftover veggies and packing them into a nutritious breakfast for the fam. It's also great for taking out and about as finger food for the little ones. I have listed specific veg ingredients here, but feel free to swap out for what you have in, the quantities don't need to be exact.

 **Makes 8 thick slices**

**Prep 12 mins, Bake 20-25 mins**

### Ingredients

1 small red pepper

1 small yellow pepper

small handful of cherry tomatoes

1 small courgette

100g (3½oz) Cheddar cheese*, grated

### From the pantry

80ml (⅓ cup) milk*

8 eggs

3 slices of bread*, stale is perfect

1 tsp garlic granules

freshly ground black pepper

Preheat the oven to 180°C fan (200°C/400°F/Gas 6) and preferably set a silicone 900g (2lb) loaf tin to one side. Or you can use a metal one, but be sure to line it with foil for easy release.

To a large bowl, add the eggs and milk and whisk very well until you see no clumps of white any more. Now cut your bread into small chunks, as small as you can, then add these to the eggs too.

Wash and dice the peppers as small as you can, chop the tomatoes into small pieces, and add to the eggs. Coarsely grate the courgette, then squeeze out as much moisture as you can over the sink before adding the veg pulp to the egg mixture too. Stir very well and finally add most of the cheese, reserving some for on the top. Add a little freshly ground black pepper and the garlic granules, then stir very well before pouring into the loaf tin. Top with the remaining cheese you set aside and bake for 40–45 minutes until puffed up, golden on top and cooked all the way through.

Allow to cool for 5 minutes before turning out onto a board and slicing. Serve to little ones in finger strips so it's easier for them to hold independently.

**Note** You can also bake these in a silicone muffin tray in the oven at 180°C fan (200°C/400°F/Gas 6) for 20–25 minutes instead to speed up the cooking time.

### ♡ Love your leftovers

Leftovers will keep in an airtight container in the fridge for up to 3 days or freeze for up to 3 months. Allow to defrost thoroughly and reheat in the oven or air fryer on HIGH for 5 minutes or 1–2 minutes in the microwave, ensuring it is piping hot before cooling a little and serving.

This recipe is perfect for using up those last few slices of stale bread, but if you don't have any available you can use 4 tablespoons of oats, or breadcrumbs too.

# Strawberry Breakfast Muffins

This makes a really big batch, perfect for brekkie and snacks all week. Or freeze for days ahead.

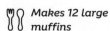

**Makes 12 large muffins**

**Prep 12 mins, Bake 20 mins**

### Ingredients

300g (10½oz) frozen strawberries

130ml (⅔ cup) plain yogurt*

### From the pantry

3 eggs*

110ml (½ cup) sunflower oil or melted unsalted butter*

30g (2½ tbsp) caster sugar (superfine) (optional)

120g (4¼oz) porridge oats*

250g self-raising flour*

1½ tsp baking powder*

Preheat the oven to 180°C fan (200°C/400°F/Gas 6) and line a deep 12-hole muffin tray with large non-stick paper cases. Or if you don't have any cases, liberally grease a muffin tray, and line the bottoms with little circles of non-stick baking paper.

Measure the strawberries into a microwaveable bowl, cover and heat on HIGH in the microwave for 2 minutes to defrost, then set aside.

In a large mixing bowl, add the yogurt, eggs, oil, and sugar, if using. Whisk together very well. Now, with the back of a fork, mash the strawberries down to a lumpy purée, it doesn't need to be smooth, and some clumps of strawberry are delicious in the finished muffins.

Add the mashed strawberries to the bowl, whisk again, then pour in the oats and stir. Sift in the flour and baking powder, then stir to incorporate into the batter. Stop mixing as soon as you see no white flour left, to avoid overworking the batter resulting in dense muffins.

Use two tablespoons to divide the batter into the muffin cases, you should get at least 2 heaped tablespoons in each case. Fill right to the brim of each section, this will give you that desired domed muffin top.

Bake for 20–25 minutes until well risen and an inserted knife comes out clean.

 **Love your leftovers**

Leftovers will store in an airtight container for 5 days, or freeze for up to 3 months. Defrost at room temperature and enjoy cold or warmed in the oven at 180°C fan (200°C/400°F/Gas 6) or air fryer at 180°C (350°F) for 5 minutes.

If you like, you can
sprinkle with a few oats
and a touch more sugar
before baking –
I like to use demerara
for a little crunch.

# Air fryer

# Cheese and Onion Bakes

GF*

EF*

DF*

V

Vg*

Scone-like in texture, these savoury bready buns are so simple to whip up, and great to enjoy on their own with some butter or paired with soup. You can swap the onion for finely shredded spring onions if you wish, or how about using a handful of washed foraged wild garlic instead if you can get your hands on some.

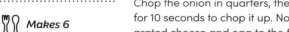

**Makes 6**

 **Prep 7 mins,**
**Bake 15-18 mins**

### Ingredients

250g (9oz) onion (approx. 2 medium onions)

80g (2¾oz) Cheddar cheese*, grated, plus a little extra for topping

#### From the pantry

200g (1½ cups) plain (all-purpose) flour*, plus a little extra for dusting

1 tsp baking powder*

1 egg*

1 tsp olive, sunflower or garlic oil

 **Love your leftovers**

Bakes will last for 3 days in an airtight container at room temperature or freeze for up to 3 months. Defrost and enjoy cold or reheat in the air fryer at 180°C (350°F) for 5 minutes until piping hot.

Chop the onion in quarters, then add to a food processor and blitz for 10 seconds to chop it up. Now add the flour, baking powder, grated cheese and egg to the food processor and whizz to combine until starting to clump together.

Take the blade out and run a spoon around to ensure all of the flour is mixed together; the dough will be slightly wet in consistency. Add a small mound of flour to a board, then press one of your palms in the flour, then with the other hand use a tablespoon to scoop out a heaped spoonful of the mixture and drop it into your floured palm. Add more flour to your other hand, then shape into a ball before pressing into a patty shape around 2cm (¾in) in thickness. Add to the air-fryer basket and repeat. A light touch here is best, to avoid overworking the dough, which would result in a dense texture, but also the patties can become very sticky and hard to handle, so quick light touches will do the trick here.

Line the air fryer with non-stick baking paper, then fill your air fryer with the bakes without them overlapping – touching on the sides is fine. You may need to cook these in batches, depending on the size of your air fryer. Drizzle over the oil, then add a tiny pinch of grated cheese to the top of each bake. Air-fry at 180°C (350°F) for 15-18 minutes until puffed up and golden on the outside.

**To cook in the oven,** shape the bakes into patties as above, then bake at 200°C fan (220°C/425°F/Gas 7) for 10–15 minutes until risen and golden.

**To fry on the hob,** shape the patties as above, but this time flatten a little more to 1cm (½in) in thickness. Add a small drizzle of oil to a large heavy-based frying pan, set over a medium heat. Add the bakes without the extra cheese on top, and fry over a medium-low heat for 5 minutes on each side until golden on the outside and fluffy inside.

**Don't have a food processor?** No problem, simply grate or chop the onion as fine as you can, add to a bowl, then stir in the rest of the ingredients.

# Carrot Chips

GF

EF

V

Crunchy in parts, soft in others, these carrot chips are so moreish, perfect as a snack on their own or a fabulous side to your main meal. These carrot chips are deliciously soft inside and a little crisp on the edges – when serving to little ones under 12 months, remove any very crispy edges for them.

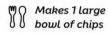 **Makes 1 large bowl of chips**

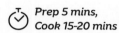 **Prep 5 mins, Cook 15-20 mins**

### Ingredients

400g (14oz) carrots

20g (¾oz) Cheddar cheese, finely grated

### From the pantry

1½ tbsp cornflour (cornstarch)

2 tsp garlic granules

½ tsp mixed dried herbs

3 tbsp sunflower, olive or garlic-infused oil

Peel the carrots, cut into thin French fry-shaped batons and put into a bowl. Add the cornflour, garlic granules and mixed herbs and toss well.

Then add the oil and mix again. Finally, add the cheese and toss again, shaking the bowl and tossing the carrots using a spoon to help the coating distribute evenly. I do this by allowing my metal spoon to reach the base of the bowl, then lifting it up through the centre of the ingredients, allowing the carrots to fall naturally, which will help the coating to roll around each carrot chip evenly.

Tumble the carrots into the air-fryer basket and cook at 190°C (375°F) for 10 minutes. Toss well and cook for a further 6–10 minutes until crisp and golden.

 **Love your leftovers**

Leftovers will keep for 2 days covered in the fridge but will need to be reheated in the air fryer at 190°C (375°F) for 5–8 minutes to crisp up again. Ensure they're piping hot in the centre before consuming. They will also freeze for 3 months, defrost thoroughly before reheating as above.

**Don't have an air fryer?**
Bake these in the oven at 180°C fan (200°C/ 400°F/Gas 6), spread out on a baking tray for 30–35 minutes.

# Smoky Sweet Potato Bites

Quick to make, and perfect to batch cook. These are delicious on their own, served with a salad or as a healthier alternative to chips next to your favourite burger!

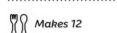 **Makes 12**

 **Prep 12 mins,
Cook 15-18 mins**

### Ingredients

350g (12oz) sweet potatoes

60g (2¼oz) Cheddar or Parmesan, grated*

### From the pantry

2 tsp garlic granules

2 tsp smoked paprika

40g (2½ tbsp) cornflour (cornstarch)

70g (2½oz) fine breadcrumbs*

1 tbsp sunflower or garlic-infused oil

freshly ground black pepper

Peel the sweet potatoes and cut into roughly 2cm (¾in) cubes. Add to a microwaveable bowl with 100ml (scant ½ cup) of water. Cover and cook on HIGH for 6 minutes. Alternatively, steam or boil on the hob until tender.

Once cooked, pour the sweet potatoes into a colander placed in the sink to drain away the water. Let the potatoes sit there for 2–3 minutes to steam away any excess moisture.

Meanwhile, to a bowl, add the garlic granules, smoked paprika, a good grinding of black pepper, the cheese and cornflour and mix. Then add the sweet potatoes and mash into the ingredients until you have a smooth purée. If it's still quite hot, leave to cool until you can handle it comfortably.

Add the breadcrumbs to a small dish, then scoop a walnut-sized amount of the mixture and add to the breadcrumbs. Toss lightly and shape into a small sausage, no need to be too precise with the shape here.

Add each bite to the base of your air-fryer basket and repeat until they're all done. It's best to avoid the bites overlapping, so do two batches if needed. Drizzle with the oil, then air-fry at 200°C (400°F) for 15–18 minutes, flipping halfway.

Serve as is, cut in half lengthways for little ones under 12 months, with your favourite dip.

 **Love your leftovers**

Leftovers will keep for 4 days in an airtight container in the fridge. To reheat, place back into the air fryer and cook at 180°C (350°F) for 5–7 minutes until crispy and piping hot. You can also freeze these for up to 3 months, place directly into the air fryer from frozen and cook at 180°C (350°F) for 10–15 minutes flipping halfway.

**Don't have an air fryer?** Bake these in the oven at 200°C fan (220°C/425°F/Gas 7) for 20 minutes, turning halfway through.

# Savoury Cheesecake Egg Cups

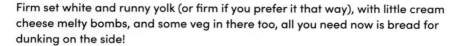

Firm set white and runny yolk (or firm if you prefer it that way), with little cream cheese melty bombs, and some veg in there too, all you need now is bread for dunking on the side!

 **Serves 1 adult and 1 little**

 **Prep 5 mins, Cook 6-13 mins**

## Ingredients

½ small red or yellow pepper, finely diced

5 tsp cream cheese*

25g (1oz) Cheddar cheese*

### From the pantry

3 eggs

sunflower or garlic-infused oil, for greasing (optional)

freshly ground black pepper

♡ **Love your leftovers**

Leftovers will keep for 2 days in an airtight container in the fridge, reheat in the air fryer at 180°C (350°F) for 3–5 minutes or until piping hot.

You can cook these two ways – in one container, or in individual ramekins or silicone muffin cases. Your cooking vessel will determine how long they will take to cook, and ideally you'll use a small enamel plate or pie dish. However, you can just use whatever you have in your kitchen. You can also use a silicone cake tin, or a ceramic baking dish. The trick is to ensure it fits inside your air fryer and that it is ovenproof and is no larger than 16cm (6¼in) diameter as this will make the eggs too thin.

Once you've chosen your equipment, assess whether it needs greasing with some oil. Silicone cookware is non-stick, so you won't need to, but if you're using ceramic, glass or enamel, give the dish a drizzle with some sunflower or garlic-infused oil.

For one large bake, crack the eggs into the dish, being careful to keep the yolks whole. Scatter over the pepper pieces, then take a teaspoon and dollop small amounts of the cream cheese over the eggs before topping with the cheese. Add a little black pepper, then carefully place in your air-fryer basket and cook at 200°C (400°F) for anywhere between 6–13 minutes. This will depend on what material and shape your dish is, and how much you want the yolk set. Ceramic high-sided containers will take longer to cook, whereas an enamel pie dish will take 6–8 minutes, so check after 6 minutes to see how runny the white is. If you would prefer a runny yolk, keep an eye on it and check every 30 seconds or so to ensure it doesn't overcook.

If you're making individual bakes, crack an egg in each one and divide the toppings between each. Air-fry at 200°C (400°F) for 7–8 minutes.

Once done, allow to cool and enjoy directly from the dish, or decant to your plate to serve alongside some bread. For littles, cut the egg into finger strips so it's easier for them to hold.

**Don't have an air fryer?** Bake in the oven at 200°C fan (220°C/425°F/Gas 7), adding a few minutes on to the cooking time.

# Crispy Paprika Fish

Delicious succulent little morsels of fish covered in a flavourful smoky coating. I've used basa fish here to keep the costs down, but you can use any flaky firm fish, depending on what's available.

**Serves 1 adult and 2 littles**

**Prep 5 mins, Cook 9-10 mins**

## Ingredients

30g (1oz) Parmesan, finely shredded

250g (9oz) skinless basa fish fillets (fresh or frozen and defrosted)

### From the pantry

40g (scant ⅓ cup) plain (all-purpose) flour*

2 tsp smoked paprika

freshly ground black pepper

Line the base of your air-fryer basket with a small sheet of baking paper to avoid sticking.

Make the flour spice mix first by adding the flour, smoked paprika and a little black pepper to a small bowl. Finely shred the Parmesan and add this too and mix until well combined.

Then cut each fish fillet into 7–8 chunky pieces and add the fillets one at a time to the flour mixture to coat well. Set aside on a plate, then add a little water to the remaining spice mix until you reach a thick but runny batter. Approx. 75ml (⅓ cup) will be needed but just add a little splash at a time and mix until you have the right consistency. Not too thick that you don't have enough but also not too runny that the batter will run off the fish.

Add the to the batter and coat well. Then place each piece in the air fryer in an even single layer, avoiding any overlapping as this will prevent them from cooking evenly. It's best that the pieces aren't tightly packed in, so you may need to cook in batches, depending on the size of your air fryer.

Then air-fry at 200°C (400°F) for 9–10 minutes until the outside crust looks dark and slightly crispy in parts. If your fillet of fish is thicker than 2cm (¾in), then you may need a little longer cooking.

I like to serve these with a little couscous and veggies, but they're also delicious made into tacos with little mini wraps, some mayo or yogurt and finely shredded lettuce. Adults add a little salt to your portion if you wish.

 **Love your leftovers**

Leftovers will keep in the fridge for 1 day, or you can freeze for up to 1 month. Defrost thoroughly in the fridge, then reheat in an air fryer at 200°C (400°F) for 5 minutes until piping hot throughout.

**Don't have an air fryer?**
You can bake these in the oven at 200°C fan (220°C/425°F/Gas 7), spread out on a lined baking tray for 10–12 minutes.

# Garlic Mushroom Twists

Flaky pastry, caramelized cheese with a soft cheesy garlic mushroom filling... These are so good, I bet you can't just have one!

 **Makes 12**

⏱ **Prep 10 mins, Cook 10-12 mins (air fry); 20-25 mins (oven)**

## Ingredients

150g (5½oz) fresh mushrooms

70g (⅓ cup) soft (cream) cheese*

1 sheet of puff pastry*

approx. 40g (1½oz) Cheddar cheese*

### From the pantry

3 garlic cloves

1 heaped tbsp cornflour (cornstarch)

freshly ground black pepper

 **Love your leftovers**

Store leftovers in an airtight container in the fridge for up to 3 days, or freeze for up to 3 months. Thaw and enjoy cold or pop in the oven at 180°C fan (200°C/350°F/Gas 4) for approx. 10 minutes until crispy and hot.

Peel and roughly chop the garlic cloves and add to a food processor to chop up finely. Cut off the dirty ends of the mushroom stalks, and wipe them clean with a piece of kitchen paper. Break each mushroom in half, then add to the food processor and blitz for 5 seconds to roughly chop.

Add the cream cheese, cornflour and a good grinding of black pepper and blitz again very briefly for approx. 6 seconds until just combined. The mushrooms should be in very small pieces now but the mixture should not be completely puréed.

Unroll the puff pastry and place landscape in front of you. Use a spatula to scrape out every last bit of the filling onto your pastry sheet, then spread evenly across the entire sheet, ensuring it is an equal thickness and reaches edge to edge.

Finely grate the Cheddar over the filling in an even layer, then fold the pastry in half lengthways, so you're left with a long rectangle, rather than a tight square. Cut the pastry into 12 equal strips, with the folded seam at one of the small ends. I find it best to place the tip of my sharp knife at the open end of the large pastry fold, then rock the blade down towards the folded side, this way the filling doesn't all squish out as you cut.

Now, one at a time, twist them by taking a pastry strip, holding an end in each hand and rotating your hands in opposite directions to form a kink in the pastry. Do this once or twice to achieve your desired finish.

To cook, place the pastries into the air-fryer basket. You don't want them to be touching and they should be at least 2cm (¾in) apart to avoid them sticking together. If the basket isn't non-stick, spray with cooking oil or line the base with non-stick baking paper. Then air-fry at 200°C (400°F) for 10–12 minutes until the pastry has turned golden brown and the filling is oozing out the sides.

Alternatively, bake on a lined baking sheet at 200°C fan (220°C/425°F/Gas 7) for 20–25 minutes until crispy, puffed up and golden.

**No food processor, no problem!** Use a knife to crush your garlic, and chop up the mushrooms nice and small before adding to a bowl and mixing in the cornflour, black pepper and cream cheese.

# Apple Crumble Pizza

 GF*

 EF

 DF*

V*

Vg*

Crisp and soft at the same time, this quick dessert is such a crowd-pleaser with minimal effort.

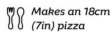 **Makes an 18cm (7in) pizza**

 **Prep 5 mins, Cook 8 mins**

## Ingredients

2 mini tortilla wraps*

1 small red eating apple

### From the pantry

20g (1½ tbsp) unsalted butter*

2 tsp vanilla extract

1 tsp sugar of choice (optional)

½ tsp ground cinnamon

3 tbsp rolled porridge oats*

Place the butter in a mug, cover and microwave for 1 minute until melted.

Meanwhile, lay one tortilla wrap on your work surface. Add 1 teaspoon of the vanilla extract and spread all over using the back of the spoon, then layer over the second tortilla, repeating again with the second teaspoon of vanilla.

Core and slice the apple as thinly as you can, ideally 2–3mm (¹⁄₁₆–⅛in) thick. Then arrange on the wraps evenly so they aren't overlapping too much.

Add the cinnamon to the melted butter, then brush over the apples and any exposed tortilla edges. There should be a small amount of butter left in the mug, add the oats and stir well to soak up the excess, then scatter these buttery oats over the apples.

Place the pizza in the air-fryer basket and air-fry at 200°C (400°F) for 8–10 minutes until golden and sizzling. Allow to cool for 3–5 minutes to allow the sizzling to settle and caramelization to crunch up a little, before cutting into triangles and enjoying. You can eat as is, or with a dollop of yogurt and fresh fruit on the side.

**To cook in the oven,** bake at 180°C fan (200°C/400°F/Gas 6) for 10–15 minutes.

 **Love your leftovers**

These will keep for 2 days in the fridge. To reheat, place in the air fryer at 180°C (350°F) or oven at 180°C fan (200°C/400°F/Gas 6) for 5–10 minutes until piping hot throughout. Or you can freeze for up to 3 months; to defrost, place in the air fryer or oven from frozen and cook for 10–15 minutes until piping hot.

# Tikka Chicken Bites

Great paired with rice, chips or on top of your favourite curry, and those leftovers are delicious in a salad. The leftovers are incredible cold too, you'll save loads of pennies making your own meat sandwich fillers.

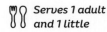 **Serves 1 adult and 1 little**

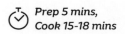 **Prep 5 mins, Cook 15-18 mins**

## Ingredients

100g (scant ½ cup) Greek yogurt*

350g (12oz) diced chicken (breast or thigh)

### From the pantry

1 tsp mixed dried herbs

2 tsp smoked paprika

1 tsp mild curry powder

1 tsp garlic granules

1 tsp oil of your choice

Add the yogurt to a large bowl, along with all the spices, mix well, then add the chicken and stir to coat. You can either cook this straight away or leave to marinate for up to 24 hours, which will intensify the flavour.

Once ready to cook, place in an even layer in the air fryer, then drizzle over the oil. Air-fry at 200°C (400°F) for 10 minutes. Flip each piece of chicken and cook again for a further 5–8 minutes until charring on the edges.

**To cook in the oven,** bake at 200°C fan (220°C/425°F/Gas 7) for 8–13 minutes.

 **Love your leftovers**

Store in an airtight container in the fridge for 3 days or freeze for 4 months. Defrost thoroughly in the fridge and consume either cold or reheated within 24 hours. To reheat, splash with a little water or oil and place back in the air fryer at 200°C (400°F) for 5–8 minutes until piping hot throughout.

# Garlic Butter Chicken Bites

GF

EF

DF*

Soft and moreish, these chicken bites are great sandwich fillers, made into tacos, on a salad, served with chips or mash, or stirred through mac and cheese.

**Serves 1 adult and 1 little**

**Prep 5 mins, Cook 12-15 mins**

## Ingredients

350g (12oz) diced chicken breasts or thighs

### From the pantry

35g (2½ tbsp) unsalted butter*

1 garlic clove, crushed (optional)

1 heaped tbsp cornflour (cornstarch)

2 tsp garlic granules

¼ tsp mixed dried herbs

freshly ground black pepper

Melt the butter in the microwave, then add the crushed garlic clove, if using, and set aside.

In a bowl, add the cornflour, garlic granules, herbs and a good grinding of black pepper. Mix well, then add the chicken and toss well to coat. Add the coated chicken to the garlic butter and stir well before adding to the air-fryer basket.

Air-fry at 200°C (400°F) for 12–15 minutes until golden on the edges and cooked through. If serving with any form of flatbread, add these to the air-fryer basket to heat up once the chicken has been removed, but there's no need to clean the basket, all those chicken juices will add lots of flavour to the bread.

**To cook in the oven,** bake at 200°C fan (220°C/425°F/Gas 7) for 8–13 minutes.

***Love your leftovers***

Store bites in an airtight container in the fridge for 3 days or freeze for 4 months. Defrost thoroughly in the fridge and consume either cold or reheated within 24 hours. To reheat, place back in the air fryer at 180°C (350°F) for 5–8 minutes until piping hot throughout.

# Garlic Green Beans

In some stores, frozen green beans are ten times cheaper than a packet of fresh, which is a real bonus when they last so much longer too. So, here's my quick way to whip up flavourful green beans, great as a side, chopped into a salad, or as a healthy snack for the kiddos.

GF*

EF

DF

V*

Vg

**Serves 1 adult and 2 littles as a side**

**Prep 2 mins, Cook 13-15 mins**

## Ingredients

300g (10½oz) frozen green beans

**From the pantry**

1½ tbsp oil, ideally garlic-infused or vegetable or sunflower oil

2 tsp garlic granules

2 tbsp dried breadcrumbs*

Tip the green beans into the air-fryer basket in an even layer. Now drizzle over the oil and quickly stir with a spoon so all the green beans are coated a little. Sprinkle over the garlic granules and breadcrumbs and stir again. Spread into an even layer and air-fry at 200°C (400°F) for 13–15 minutes, stirring halfway though.

Once done they will be soft in parts and crisp in others and the speckles of breadcrumbs will have turned golden. Feel free to cook longer if you prefer a crispier texture.

Serve as is to little ones, with a sprinkle of salt for us adults.

If you only have fresh green beans, follow the same method but cook for 8–10 minutes instead.

 **Love your leftovers**

Any leftovers will keep in the fridge for 2 days. Reheat in the air fryer at 180°C (350°F) for 5 minutes until piping hot or enjoy cold. You can freeze for up to 2 months if you wish, but they are best served fresh.

I like to give these to Nina for her after school snack, and if she eats a little bowl before dinner, any veg she does eat with her meal is a bonus.

# Sweet and Sour Wings

Crispy chicken wings coated in a Chinese-inspired sweet and sour sauce. Finger-licking good!

**Serves 2 adults and 2 littles as part of a meal**

**Prep 10 mins, Cook 20 mins**

## Ingredients

750g (1lb 10oz) chicken wings

1–2 large oranges or approx. 110ml (½ cup) orange juice

...............

### From the pantry

2 tbsp cornflour (cornstarch)

1 tsp baking powder*

approx. 1 tbsp sunflower oil

35g (2 tbsp) unsalted butter*

1 large garlic clove, crushed

15g (1 tbsp) honey or caster sugar (superfine) (optional)

2 tbsp low-salt soy sauce*

1 tsp sesame oil (optional)

freshly ground black pepper

If they aren't already, halve each chicken wing down the centre joint using a big sharp knife. To do this, with the skin side down on the board, place your knife blade over the knuckle joint in the middle of a chicken wing, you should feel the knife being able to cut through. If it can't, you've hit the bone, so try again closer to where you see the joint through the skin. Add the cornflour and baking powder to a bowl, and stir to incorporate, then add all the wings and toss to coat.

Add the floured wings to your air-fryer basket and drizzle the oil over the top. Air-fry at 200°C (400°F) for 20 minutes, tossing halfway through.

While the wings cook, make the sauce. Juice the orange into a small saucepan, measuring how much you have got. It should be around 110ml (½ cup), if it's less by much more, add another orange, just a little should be fine.

Add the butter, garlic, honey or sugar, if using, soy sauce and sesame oil, if using, along with a good grinding of black pepper. Give it a good stir and set over a medium heat to boil for approx. 5 minutes. Stir often to avoid sticking, then once the mixture has drastically reduced to a thick sauce, remove from the heat and set aside.

Once the wings are crispy (they will look a little white from the flour but this is fine), toss into a serving bowl and pour the sauce on top. Give them a stir to coat well.

Serve as is, adults, add a little extra salt to your portion. For little ones under 2, you can remove the meat from the bone if you wish, it will be super tender and juicy, or let them dig in and nibble away at a wing on their own. Choose the drumstick-shaped wings if you go for this method.

 **Love your leftovers**

Leftovers will keep for 3 days in the fridge. Reheat in an ovenproof bowl with an extra small splash of water and drizzle of oil to keep the outside sauce succulent, covered with some foil, in an oven preheated to 200°C fan (220°C/425°F/Gas 7) for 20 minutes until piping hot inside. You can freeze any leftovers, defrosting thoroughly before reheating as above.

# Broccoli and Bacon Quiche

GF*

DF*

V*

With a handful of humble ingredients, you have lunch or dinner ready in no time. I've used a tortilla wrap here for the base, but feel free to swap for puff, short or even layered filo pastry for a more substantial crust.

**1 adult and 2 littles**

**Prep 10 mins, Bake 12–15 mins**

## Ingredients

4 thin slices of bacon* (optional)

5 broccoli florets

1 large tortilla wrap*

approx. 20g (¾oz) Cheddar cheese*, finely grated

### From the pantry

4 eggs

approx. 40ml (2⅔ tbsp) milk*

freshly ground black pepper

**Love your leftovers**

Leftover quiche will last for 2 days in the fridge or you can freeze it for up to 3 months. Defrost thoroughly and reheat in the air fryer at 180°C (350°F) for 5–8 minutes until piping hot.

If you're adding bacon to your quiche, chop into small lardon pieces and add to the air-fryer basket, then cook at 200°C (400°F) for 6 minutes.

While that cooks, prepare the quick filling. Finely shred the broccoli with a knife or pair of kitchen scissors, using mostly just the dark green ends as these cook much quicker. Reserve the stalks to add to soups or stews.

To a bowl, crack in the eggs, ideally weighing them. It should reach approx. 210ml (scant 1 cup), add enough milk to bring this volume up to 250ml (generous 1 cup). If you don't have any scales, don't worry, just add the 40ml (2⅔ tbsp) of milk, it will still work just fine, then whisk very well. Add the broccoli and black pepper to the eggs and milk and mix again.

Once the bacon is done, lift out the air-fryer basket and spoon it into the eggs. Immediately stir the mixture to stop the egg from cooking. Add the tortilla wrap to the base of the air-fryer basket, doing this as neatly as possible, so that the wrap comes up the side of the basket a little at the same height all the way around. If the tortilla doesn't come at least 1.5cm (⅝in) up the sides of the basket you run the risk of the filling spilling out.

Now pour in the egg mixture, top with a light layer of grated cheese and air-fry at 200°C (400°F) for 12–15 minutes. You'll know it's done when the top has turned golden, and when pressed the egg feels firm and not too squidgy, which would indicate there's still raw egg underneath. If you're using pastry for the base, drizzle a little oil over the exposed pastry, then air-fry for 15–20 minutes instead.

**To cook in the oven,** place the tortilla wrap in a small round cake tin, small enough that the wrap will come up the sides. Fill as above and bake for 15–20 minutes at 180°C fan (200°C/400°F/ Gas 6) until the egg has set.

# Banana Chelsea Buns

Quick to whip up, these are perfect if you and the gang fancy a warming sweet treat. Very low in sugar, so I definitely wouldn't shy away from serving these for breakfast too!

**Makes 5**

**Prep 10 mins,
Bake 15 mins**

## Ingredients

100g (3½oz) raisins or
currants (optional)

1 large banana

### From the pantry

2 tsp ground cinnamon

2 tsp light soft brown
sugar (optional)

200g (1½ cups) self-
raising flour*, plus extra
for dusting if needed

1 tsp baking powder*

100ml (scant ½ cup) milk*,
plus extra (optional) for
brushing

30ml (2 tbsp) melted
unsalted butter, or
sunflower oil*, plus extra
(optional) for brushing

Roughly chop the dried fruit, then mash the banana in a bowl using the back of a fork. Add the cinnamon, sugar, if using, and chopped raisins. Stir and set aside to let the raisins plump up a little.

In a mixing bowl, add the flour, baking powder, milk and melted butter or oil. Stir until it comes together to a dough and tip out onto a clean work surface. Gently and briefly knead the mixture together into a ball of dough, ensuring to not press down firmly or overwork the dough as this will result in a chewy, dense bun.

Roll the dough out to a rough rectangle shape, dusting the surface with flour if needed. There's no need to get the tape measure out, but you want a long rectangle shape, with the short edge approx. 13cm (5in) in length and approx. 1cm (½in) thick, thinner will result in more layers to the spiral.

Spread your banana mixture edge to edge over the dough, ensuring the raisins are evenly placed. Cut the dough sheet into 5 long strips, I find using a pizza cutter best for this, then roll up into spirals.

Line your air-fryer basket with non-stick baking paper, then place each bun, spiral side up, in the basket, not too tightly touching. If there's any pieces of raisin sticking up, press them between the layers, or remove as these will catch and burn during cooking.

Brush the exposed dough with either melted butter, milk or sunflower oil, then air-fry at 180°C (400°F) for 10–15 minutes until puffed up and golden, but check after 8 minutes to see how they're doing in case they are browning early, all air fryers are different. We love them just as is, but you can add a little water icing drizzle if you wish.

 **Love your leftovers**

If you have any leftovers, store in an airtight container for 3 days, but do note they are nicest on the day of baking and will harden a little as time goes on. You can also freeze these and bake from frozen. Add a splash of water and bake in the air fryer at 200°C (400°F) for 10 minutes, or until defrosted and reheated throughout.

GF*
EF
DF*
V
Vg*

**Don't have an air fryer?**
Bake these Chelsea buns in the oven at 180°C fan (200°C/400°F/Gas 6) for 20–25 minutes.

# Bread and Butter Pudding

Fancy a comforting classic pud without putting the oven on? This is the one for you!

GF*

DF*

V*

Vg*

Take a heatproof dish that fits in your air fryer, or use the air fryer's removable non-stick compartment. Ensure it has no holes in it as this will not work. All brands of air fryers are different, so use whichever method is going to give you the biggest space possible.

**Serves 2 adults and 2 littles**

Take a piece of non-stick baking paper, large enough to line your compartment, and crumple it completely into a ball in your hands, this will help it mould easier. Then unravel it and begin to line the vessel you're going to cook your bread and butter pud in.

**Prep 10 mins, Bake 20-22 mins**

In a bowl, crack in the eggs and add the milk, sugar if using, and vanilla extract. Whisk really well until the egg is completely whisked into the liquid. If using standard sliced bread, butter each side of the bread. Then cut or tear your chosen bread into 2.5–5cm (1–2in) chunks and add to your lined dish.

## Ingredients

approx. 400g (14oz) stale leftover bread* (I love to use stale croissants and brioche rolls for this)

Pour over the egg mixture, and press the bread pieces down into the liquid to saturate. Leave to stand for 5 minutes or as long as you can wait, then put into the air fryer and cook at 180°C (350°F) for 20–22 minutes.

### From the pantry

250ml (generous 1 cup) milk*

3 eggs or store-bought vegan egg replacer*

3 tbsp caster sugar (superfine) (optional)

2 tsp vanilla extract

approx. 2 tbsp butter* (leave out if using croissants or brioche)

To check the pudding is done, gently lift one side of the baking paper and use a spoon to edge the pudding away from the side. If you see some runny milk/egg mixture, it's not done yet, so cook for another 3–5 minutes and check again.

Once done, allow to stand for approx. 5 minutes to cool and harden a touch, then enjoy.

**For extra deliciousness,** add approx. 50g (1¾oz) of chopped chocolate between the bread layers, ensuring none is sticking up on top, this will melt and ooze into the pudding, such a win! And/or try adding a mashed banana into the egg mixture for a delicious fruity sweetness.

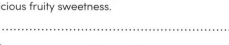

### ♡ Love your leftovers

Leftovers will keep for 3 days in the fridge, place back in the air fryer for 10 minutes to reheat until piping hot through to enjoy warm again, or it can be eaten cold if you can't wait.

# Fussy eaters

# Nostalgic Tomato Pasta

This sauce will have you coming back for more. Smooth and silky, which reminds you of old school tomato soup, utterly delicious and a real comfort dinner in a hurry.

GF*

EF

DF*

V*

Vg*

 **Serves 2 adults and 2 littles**

**Prep and cook 10 mins**

## Ingredients

1 large carrot

### From the pantry

250g (9oz) pasta*

500g (1lb 2oz) passata

1 tsp caster sugar (superfine) (optional)

1 low-salt chicken or vegetable stock cube*

2 tsp smoked paprika

40g (scant 3 tbsp) unsalted butter*

Set a large pan of boiling water over a high heat. While you wait for it to come to the boil, peel the carrot and cut into chunky discs.

When the water is boiling, add the pasta, stir and cook according to the packet instructions.

To make the sauce, set a lidded saucepan over a medium-high heat, and pour in the passata, trying to get every last drop into the pan. Now add the carrot, the sugar, if using, this really helps cut through the sourness that comes from the tomatoes. Crumble in the stock cube in small pieces, then add the smoked paprika. Give it a really good stir and allow it to come to a low simmer. Cook until the pasta is done, stirring often, and keeping the lid on, but resting ajar on the side to allow steam to escape. You want the sauce to reduce by a third at least, so do allow moisture to evaporate, but the sauce will splatter a little, so to save on cleaning your kitchen, keep the pot partially covered.

Once the pasta is done, quickly add the butter to the sauce and stir to help it melt. Then drain the pasta and add to the sauce. If you can keep a little of the pasta cooking, that is ideal so you can thin the consistency of the sauce if needed.

Serve as is, with or without the carrot, we love a little grated cheese on top but it's delicious without too. Adults, you may want to add some salt to your portion as well.

♡ **Love your leftovers**

This dish is best served fresh, however, if you have some left over, I recommend pouring into an ovenproof dish and storing in the fridge. This will keep for 2 days, then when you'd like to enjoy, add a splash of water, a little grated cheese on top and bake for 20–25 minutes until golden and crisp and piping hot throughout.

# Turkey Chilli

 GF*

 EF

DF

Vg*

V*

Turkey mince is often cheaper than beef mince when comparing the same quality. It is also lower in saturated fat, making this chilli a much healthier version. However, if you'd prefer, swap for lean minced beef for a more authentic dish.

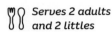 **Serves 2 adults and 2 littles**

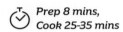 **Prep 8 mins, Cook 25-35 mins**

## Ingredients

1 medium onion (optional)

500g (1lb 2oz) minced turkey or chicken (or plant-based mince)*

### From the pantry

1 tbsp sunflower oil

2 tsp ground cumin

2 tsp garlic granules

3 tsp smoked paprika

1 low-salt chicken or beef stock cube*

1 tsp mixed dried herbs

280g (9½oz) frozen sweetcorn or unsalted canned

400g (14oz) can of kidney beans in water (salt free)

400g (14oz) can of chopped tomatoes freshly ground black pepper

Set a large lidded saucepan over a medium heat, and add the sunflower oil. Meanwhile, if using, dice the onion as small as you can, or alternatively grate on the coarse side of a box grater if you'd prefer the onion to be hidden within the dish.

Add the onion to the pan, and sauté for approx. 3 minutes, stirring often until it starts to turn translucent. Now add the mince, and begin to break it up with a wooden spoon, stirring well. Cook for a further 3 minutes, continuing to break up the meat into smaller chunks as it cooks.

Once you can see no pink meat, add the ground cumin, garlic granules, smoked paprika, a good grinding of black pepper, the stock cube and mixed herbs. Stir really well, then tip in the sweetcorn, kidney beans, including the water in the tin, and the chopped tomatoes. Give it a really good stir, then pop the lid on, turn the heat down to low and cook for 20–30 minutes. Give it a stir every so often to distribute the flavours well and avoid it sticking to the base of the pan, you can add a dash of water as needed if it's starting to get too dry.

Serve with rice and avocado if you have it, or a simple salad also works amazingly. Don't forget the grated cheese to melt on the hot chilli on your plate, the best bit!

**Slow cooker** Alternatively, this chilli can be made in a slow cooker. Brown the mince in a frying pan before adding to the slow cooker with the remaining ingredients. Opt for grated onion here as it blends into the sauce nicely when cooked in the slow cooker. Stir really well, pop the lid on and cook on HIGH for 3 hours or LOW for 6–8 hours.

 *Love your leftovers*

This chilli will last for 2 days in an airtight container in the fridge, or freeze for up to 3 months. Thaw thoroughly before reheating in a saucepan until bubbling and piping hot throughout.

If serving to under-2s, mash or blitz the kidney beans before adding to the pan, as large beans can pose a choking hazard for little eaters.

# Family-friendly Nacho Night

Nachos are usually made using salty and very crunchy corn crisps, delicious but not ideal for little ones. This version lets you make your own tortilla chips to determine the saltiness and texture of the dish, making it suitable for all ages.

GF*

EF

DF*

**2 adults and 1 little**

**Prep 10 mins, Bake 10-15 mins**

## Ingredients

8 mini tortilla wraps, or 6 large ones*

5 or 6 salad tomatoes

Turkey Chilli (see page 102)

### From the pantry

approx. 1 tbsp sunflower oil

1 garlic clove

freshly ground black pepper

### To serve

handful of grated cheese of your choice*

3 tbsp sour cream or thick Greek plain yogurt*

chilli sauce, for the adults

---

Preheat the oven to 180°C fan (200°C/400°F/Gas 6).

Stack the tortilla wraps and cut into 8 small triangles like you're slicing a cake. If you're using large tortilla wraps, cut into 8 triangles, then cut each triangle in half, so all the pieces are roughly the same size.

Add half the tortilla pieces to a large baking tray and spread out into an even layer. Drizzle with a little oil, then add the remaining tortilla spreading out to an even layer too. Try to avoid too much overlapping, as this will prevent them from crisping up. Drizzle over a little more oil, then pop the tray in the oven. If you're serving to little ones under 2, remove the tortillas after 10–12 minutes of cooking, once they have taken on a little colour and crisped up a little, but are still soft in most parts, these are perfect for little taste testers. Adults, you can pop yours back in the oven for longer if you wish.

If serving to families who can handle a little more crunch, bake your tortillas for 13–16 minutes until most of the tortilla pieces are golden brown and visibly crunchy.

While your tortillas bake, make your tomato salsa. Cut one tomato in half, then, using the fine side of a cheese grater, place the cut side on the grid and grate the tomato onto a board or into your serving bowl. It will turn into a runny tomato pulp, this is the base for the salsa. You should be left with the skin in your fingers, discard this. Now peel the garlic clove and grate this on the fine grater too. Depending on the size of your garlic clove, either grate the whole thing or just half, depending on your taste, but remember we're not cooking this, so the taste will be stronger than usual.

**Recipe continues on page 106**

With your remaining tomatoes, use a serrated knife to cube them as small as you can; the smaller the pieces, the more sauce-like the salsa will be. Add these to the grated tomato in a small serving bowl, along with a little freshly ground black pepper to taste, mix really well and set aside.

Once your tortilla chips are done, either add a small amount to each person's plate, or add them all to a serving platter. Now add your hot turkey chilli to the centre of your nacho pile, spreading out a little to create more surface area. Quickly add the grated cheese so it can begin melting.

You can pop this back into the oven for a few minutes to melt, but I like to simply cover with a little foil and wait a few moments, the excess chilli heat will help melt that cheese. Add your salsa and cream cheese, if using, along with any other toppings you wish – chopped avocado is delicious too, or you can whizz it up for a quick and easy guacamole.

If you feel your tortilla chips have gone a little too crunchy for your baba, simply submerge a few chips in the hot chilli for 5 minutes, this will soak up lots of the chilli sauce, softening the tortilla chip.

. . . . . . . . . . . . . . . . . . . . . . . . . . . . . . . . . . . . . . . . . . . . . . . . . . . . . . . . . .

 *Love your leftovers*

This dish is best served fresh, however, baked tortilla chips that haven't been layered with other ingredients can be kept in an airtight container for a day.

# Simple Chicken and Leek Pie

Top this gorgeous classic pie with cheesy mashed potato, sliced spuds, shortcrust pastry or our favourite puff pastry is always a win in my house.

GF*

EF*

DF*

**Serves 3 adults and 2 littles**

**Prep 20 mins, Bake 25-30 mins**

## Ingredients

4–6 boneless chicken thighs

400g (14oz) leeks (2 medium leeks)

2 heaped tbsp cream cheese* (optional)

1 sheet of ready-rolled puff pastry*

**From the pantry**

2 tbsp sunflower oil

2 low-salt chicken stock cubes*

250ml (generous 1 cup) milk*

2 large garlic cloves, crushed

1 heaped tbsp cornflour (cornstarch)

1 small egg or milk*, for brushing

freshly ground black pepper

Preheat the oven to 200°C fan (220°C/425°F/Gas 7).

Heat large heavy-based frying pan with 1 tablespoon of oil. While it comes up to temperature, cut the chicken into bite-sized chunks or strips, then add to the pan in an even layer. Season with a little black pepper and allow to gain some colour, browning for 5 minutes.

Meanwhile, trim the leeks, then very finely chop into small pieces, as small as you can. If your little ones don't mind larger leek chunks, don't worry about going too fine. You could briefly blitz in a blender if you find this easier. Then put into a colander and wash very well, as sometimes leeks have some hidden dirt between the layers. (If you're using a blender, I would wash the leeks first.) Shake well to drain off the excess water and set aside.

Once the chicken has browned all over, transfer the meat to an ovenproof ceramic or enamel dish, reserving any cooking juices in the pan. Add a touch more oil if it needs it, then add the leeks. Sauté for approx. 4 minutes until soft and most of the liquid has evaporated. While the leeks cook, boil the kettle with a little water and measure 250ml (generous 1 cup) into a jug, crumbling in the stock cubes. Now top up to 500ml (generous 2 cups) with milk for a creamier sauce.

Once the leeks are soft, add another tablespoon of oil, or a knob of butter if you have it, along with the garlic, then sprinkle over the mounded tablespoon of cornflour into the leeks. Stir and cook for a couple of minutes, before gradually adding the milky stock. Add a little to start with and use a wooden spoon to stir vigorously, helping the flour clumps melt into the sauce, keep adding little by little and soon all the flour will dissolve and you'll have a smooth sauce. Add the remaining milk, stir and bring to a simmer.

**Recipe continues on page 109**

Spoon in the cream cheese and let it melt into the sauce, then allow it all to simmer away for 5 minutes until thickened. Pour into your ovenproof dish to join the chicken, stirring well to coat the meat in the sauce.

Now top with your desired topping, I've gone for pastry here as it's our fave. Lay the pastry over the dish and gently seal on the edges. Trim the excess, if you have lots left over, re-roll back up and store in the fridge for another recipe. If there's only a small amount, I like to make little shapes for the top, or even our family's initials to decorate if I have time. Brush the pastry with a little beaten egg or milk, glueing any decorations down with this wash and adding more on top too.

Cut a small cross in the centre of the pie approx. 2.5cm (1in) in size, this lets the steam escape, then bake for 25–30 minutes until puffed up and golden.

If you like, you can use frozen leeks here, but defrost them first and chop finely.

 **Love your leftovers**

Leftovers will keep for 2 days in the fridge or freeze for 3 months. Defrost thoroughly and reheat in an oven preheated to 200°C fan (220°C/425°F/Gas 7) for 15–20 minutes until bubbling and piping hot throughout.

# Leftover Roast Crispy Quesadillas

 GF*

 EF

 DF*

When I made this quick whip-up dinner for my Nina in a hurry one spring evening, I did not expect her to absolutely devour these like there's no tomorrow. At first she refused them, but then she watched me enjoy my portion and gave it a go. "Mum please put this in your book, it's so good!"

 **Serves 1 adult and 2 littles**

🕐 **Prep and cook 10 mins**

## Ingredients

approx. 200g (7oz) cooked chicken*

2 large flour tortillas*

60g (2¼oz) Cheddar cheese*, grated

### From the pantry

2 tbsp sunflower or garlic-infused oil

2 tbsp low-salt soy sauce*

1 tsp smoked paprika

1 tsp garlic granules

freshly ground black pepper

Shred the chicken, then add to a large, preheated frying pan with 1 tablespoon of oil. Fry for a few minutes, stirring often until it is starting to reheat and gain a little colour on the edges. Add the soy sauce, smoked paprika, garlic granules and black pepper, then stir and toss well. The chicken should soften with the moisture of the soy sauce. Keep cooking for a further 2 minutes until piping hot.

On a board, lay the two tortillas flat next to each other. On one half of each, add a small sprinkling of cheese, then spoon the chicken mixture over the top of the cheese, spreading to the edge of the semicircle in an even layer. Add another small handful of cheese on top of the chicken and fold over the clean side of each tortilla so you have two filled semicircles of quesadilla wraps.

Place the empty frying pan over a medium heat, there's no need to clean it. Then drizzle in the remaining tablespoon of oil. Add a small sprinkling of cheese to the pan. Quickly and confidently, lift each quesadilla into the pan, slotting together so the folded sides are down the centre of the pan.

Sprinkle a little more cheese on top, then cook for a few minutes until golden on the underneath. Flip over, then cook for a further couple of minutes until crisp and golden on each side.

Place on a large chopping board, cut into 4 or 5 triangles and allow to settle for a couple more minutes to firm up before serving alongside a picky salad for a quick and easy meal.

 **Love your leftovers**

Leftovers will keep for 24 hours – store in the fridge if planning to keep longer than a couple of hours. To gain crispiness again, pop back into a frying pan over a low heat until crispy on both sides.

This recipe is great for using up any leftover cooked meat. Or you can use a large handful of sliced mushrooms, grated courgette, or chopped peppers.

# Rebecca's Sloppy Joes

GF*

EF

DF*

My version of this American classic is quick, cheap, with hidden extra veggies inside, and easy to make, but the best part is that it's not so sloppy, just the right amount, and it's delicious! Head to page 114 to find out what to do with your leftovers, if you have any that is!

 **Makes 6–8 sandwiches**

 **Prep 5 mins, Cook 20 mins**

## Ingredients

500g (1lb 2oz) minced (ground) beef (5–10% fat), or plant-based mince

1 large brown onion

1 large courgette (zucchini)

soft bread rolls, buttered*, to serve

grated cheese*, to serve

### From the pantry

2 garlic cloves

1 tsp sugar (optional)

2 tbsp tomato purée (paste)

1 low-salt beef stock cube*

2 tbsp low-salt soy sauce*

1 tbsp Worcestershire sauce*

1 tsp smoked paprika

freshly ground black pepper

In a large, wide frying pan set over a high heat, add the meat and break up with a wooden spoon. Cook for 5 minutes, breaking up the meat chunks and stirring often to brown thoroughly and caramelize at the edges.

While the meat fries, prepare the onion. You can peel and finely dice if you wish, but I prefer to grate it so the onion turns into a purée and melts into the dish, resulting in a less noticeable finish, perfect for fussy little ones. Now grate the courgette before turning the box grater around and finally grating the garlic cloves on the fine grate side. Add all of this to the mince, stir really well and cook for a further 4–5 minutes.

Add the sugar, if using, tomato purée, crumbled beef stock cube, soy sauce, Worcestershire sauce, smoked paprika and a good grinding of black pepper, stir and cook for a further 10 minutes. Every so often, stir the mince, scraping it all around off the base of the pan, then flatten again in an even layer with the back of your wooden spoon. This will help the edges caramelize and gain lots of flavour, but do remember to stir every couple of minutes as these edges will catch if left too long. If you feel it's a little too dry, add splashes of water between each stir to add a little more moisture, but be careful not to add too much to turn it sloppy. If you do, simply cook for longer until the water evaporates.

It will be done once the colour has darkened a little and the mince smells amazing.

To serve, spoon your desired amount inside a buttered roll, top with a little grated cheese allowing it to melt a little from the heat of the mince, and serve with salad on the side.

**Leftovers** will keep covered in the fridge for 3 days or freeze for up to 4 months. Defrost thoroughly, then reheat in a saucepan with an extra splash of water to loosen the consistency.

# Leftover Sloppy Joes Pasta

GF*
EF
DF*

Wondering what to do with your leftover Sloppy Joes minced meat? Well, turn it into a whole new dish, loaded with extra veggies in this creamy and comforting leftover pasta dish. If you didn't make Sloppy Joes yesterday and fancy this meal today, simply follow the instructions on how to make the mince on page 112, then after adding the spices, follow the instructions below.

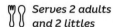

**Serves 2 adults and 2 littles**

**Cook 10 mins**

## Ingredients

1 courgette (zucchini), grated

approx. 250g (9oz) Sloppy Joes mince (see page 112)

100g (½ cup) soft cream cheese*

70g (2½oz) Cheddar cheese*, grated

### From the pantry

200ml (scant 1 cup) milk*

250g (9oz) pasta*

1 tbsp sunflower oil or butter*

Set a large pot of boiling water over a high heat and add the pasta. Cook according to the packet instructions.

Meanwhile, add the oil or butter to a large frying pan over a high heat. Add the grated courgette and cook for 2 minutes, stirring a little until softened. Now add your leftover Sloppy Joes meat, and press down into the courgette, stirring well. Allow this to cook and reheat for a few minutes before gradually adding the milk. Stir well and allow this to create a creamier, softer-textured sauce.

Once piping hot throughout and bubbling a little at the sides, add the cream cheese and stir well to incorporate into the sauce. If you need to, add a small ladle of the pasta cooking water to loosen the sauce. Once well combined, turn the heat off, add the grated cheese and stir once more to allow it to melt.

Now the pasta should be cooked, drain and add to the sauce, stirring really well. We like it served just like this with some extra greens on the side, but if you wish you can spoon it all into a baking dish, top with a little more cheese and bake in the oven at 200°C fan (220°C/425°F/Gas 7) for 20 minutes until the top is crispy and golden.

## ♡ Love your leftovers

This dish is best eaten straight away to avoid reheating the meat more than once. If you feel that 250g (9oz) will be too much for one sitting, allow approx. 80g (2¾oz) of dried pasta for each adult and approx. half the amount for each little, but this amount is simply a guide, all little ones have very different appetites, which is completely normal.

# Sesame Mushroom Chinese Pork

Quick to whip up, this gorgeous pork dish can be used in so many ways, a recipe staple to have under your belt. You can use chicken, beef or turkey mince too.

GF*

EF

DF

 **Serves 2 adults and 1 little**

 **Prep 5 mins, Cook 15 mins**

## Ingredients

500g (1lb 2oz) 5–10% fat pork mince

250g (9oz) closed cup or chestnut mushrooms

### From the pantry

drizzle of sunflower oil, for cooking

2 tsp sesame oil

2 garlic cloves, crushed

1 tsp caster sugar (superfine) (optional)

2 tbsp reduced-salt soy sauce*

2 tbsp sesame seeds

Set a large nonstick frying pan over a medium-high heat and drizzle with a little oil for cooking. Add the pork mince and break up with a spatula to brown the meat all over. While the pork cooks, brush off any dirt from the mushrooms and slice or cube into small pieces.

Keep cooking the pork until it's charred and crispy in some areas, flattening it down with a spatula to increase the surface area of cooking. After a minute or so, stir again and flatten again, so that the meat gets crispy quicker. After 6 minutes, it should be fully cooked and charred on some edges, but generally still pale looking.

Add the mushrooms, sesame oil, garlic, sugar if using, soy sauce and sesame seeds and stir well. Cook for a further 5–8 minutes, stirring and flattening for a minute or so as before to help the pork and mushrooms turn crispy and jammy.

Serve alongside some sticky rice or inside warmed flatbreads. I like to have this with finely shredded or sliced carrots drizzled with a little sesame oil. Adults, add some chilli oil and a little more soy to your portion to ramp up the flavour.

 **Love your leftovers**

Leftovers will keep in an airtight container in the fridge for 3 days or freeze for up to 3 months. Defrost thoroughly, then reheat in a frying pan for 5–6 minutes until piping hot. Add a splash of water to add some moisture back into the dish.

Sesame
Mushroom Chinese
Pork (see page 116),
Sesame Mushroom Pork
Noodles (see page 118),
Sesame Mushroom
Pork Fried Rice
(see page 119)

# Sesame Mushroom Pork Noodles

Silky noodles in a flavourful sesame pork sauce with cabbage for extra greens (pictured on page 117, top).

 **Prep 7 mins, Cook 15 mins**

### Ingredients

200g (7oz) medium egg noodles

pork ingredients as on page 116

⅓ head of sweetheart cabbage or Chinese leaf

spring onions (scallions), to serve (optional)

### From the pantry

1 tbsp cornflour (cornstarch)

Set a pan of boiling water over a high heat and cook the noodles according to the packet instructions. Once the noodles are done, drain and set aside.

Cook the pork and mushrooms as on page 116. While the pork is cooking initially, wash the cabbage, then, using a sharp knife or box grater, finely shred the cabbage. Try to get it as thin as you can so it will melt into the sauce.

When you add the mushrooms and extra flavours to the pork, also add the shredded cabbage. Stir, cook and toss for 10 minutes until the pork is charred and the cabbage is soft.

Add the cornflour to a small bowl or cup and add 3 tablespoons of water, stir to form a paste, then top up with 100ml of water, stirring well to dissolve. Add all this to the pork and stir well, it should thicken instantly. Now you have a sauce, add the noodles and toss to coat the mince sauce around the noodles. If you prefer a saucier consistency, add a touch more boiling water from the kettle and toss to combine.

Serve with a few optional slices of spring onion, with a little more soy sauce for us adults.

# Sesame Mushroom Pork Fried Rice

This pork was made to be transformed into a fried rice dish. So flavourful and comforting, the perfect Friday night fakeaway (pictured on page 117, bottom left).

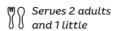

**Serves 2 adults and 1 little**

**Prep 5 mins, Cook 20 mins**

### Ingredients

pork ingredients as on page 116

250g (9oz) packet ready-cooked microwave long-grain rice

**From the pantry**

2 eggs

Make the pork dish as on page 116 until jammy and charred in parts, then take the unheated rice and crumble it in the packet before adding to the pork. Stir and cook for a further 3 minutes until the rice is piping hot and soft throughout.

Now make a hole in the centre of the pan, pushing the rice and pork to the sides. Crack the eggs into a bowl, whisk and tip into the hole you've just made. With a spatula, quickly stir and whisk the eggs until 75% cooked, then start to bring in the rice and pork to cook all together. Stir everything very well, scraping the bottom of the pan with the spatula to stir and cook evenly. After a minute or so, serve up into bowls with a little cucumber on the side. Adults add a dash more soy sauce to your portion.

♡ **Love your leftovers**

If you've made these recipes using leftovers from page 116 (Sesame mushroom chinese pork), then it's best to eat them straight away as you've already reheated the pork.

# Sesame Mushroom Pork Toastie

Got some leftover pork and want to make it into a new meal? This is what you gotta do! Eggy bread sides, soft meat filling with a crispy sesame crust.

 **Makes**
**1 toastie**

**Prep 4 mins,**
**Cook 6 mins**

## Ingredients

3 heaped tbsp leftover
pork mixture (see above)

2 slices of bread*

30g (1oz) Cheddar
cheese*, grated

### From the pantry

1 egg

oil, for cooking

1 tbsp sesame seeds

Add the leftover pork to a small microwaveable bowl, cover and heat on HIGH for 2 minutes to take the cold fridge edge off it and ensure we are thoroughly reheating the meat when making the toastie.

Then make a sandwich with the leftover pork and the grated cheese. In a large flat-bottomed bowl, add the egg and whisk well. Dip the sandwich into the beaten egg, flipping over so both sides are soaked.

Take a non-stick frying pan and drizzle with a little oil over a medium-low heat. Sprinkle the top side of the egg-soaked sandwich with ½ tablespoon of sesame seeds. Then pick up the sandwich and place in the pan, sesame-seed side down. Sprinkle the other side with the remaining sesame seeds as this will be facing up in the pan now. Cook the toastie for 4–6 minutes, flipping after a couple of minutes until both sides are browned, the egg is cooked through and the cheese inside is melted. Be sure to avoid burning the seeds, so if they are browning too quickly, turn the heat down and put a lid on the pan, which will help the cheese inside melt quicker.

Cut into finger strips for little ones, or in half for us big kids. Enjoy with a little side salad if you wish.

**Note** This dish is best eaten straight away as the meat has been reheated.

# Butter-free Scones

GF*

DF*

V

With the rising cost of ingredients, butter being one of the hardest hit, these scones cost that little bit less to make by replacing the butter with oil, which not only makes these delicious treats cheaper, but also quicker and easier to make (pictured on page 124, bottom).

🍴 **Makes
8-15**

⏱ **Prep 5 mins,
Bake 13-17 mins**

## Ingredients

**From the pantry**

160ml (¾ cup) milk*

350g (2⅔ cups)
self-raising flour*

1 tsp baking powder*

3 tbsp sunflower or
vegetable oil

1 egg

Preheat the oven to 200°C fan (220°C/425°F/Gas 7).

Measure the flour and baking powder into a bowl, stir and make a well in the centre. Now take a jug, measure in the oil, milk and add the egg. Whisk together well, then pour into the flour mixture, stirring straight away with a metal tablespoon. As the mixture comes together, use a folding action where you rotate the bowl and scoop the mixture from the base of the bowl upwards to lightly fold the ingredients together, avoiding vigorously stirring as you run the risk of overworking the dough.

Once you see the mixture pretty much coming together (this should take approx. 20 seconds), tip the contents out onto a clean, floured work surface. Using your hands, gently pat and squeeze the dough together but don't knead it. The trick here is to lightly work the dough and avoid pressing it together too much as this will result in flat scones.

Bring the dough into a circle and pat down to approx. 3cm (1¼in) in thickness, the thicker the dough, the better the rise. If it's a little flaky on top don't worry, we'll fix that in the next step.

Use a round cutter, ideally 7cm (2¾in) in diameter, to cut out the scones and transfer to a lined baking dish.

Add a splash of milk to the empty bowl you used to whisk the egg, oil and milk together. Then use your fingers to very gently pat some milk on to the top of each scone, being careful not to let any liquid fall down the sides as this also prevents a high rise. Here you can make sure any flaky pieces of dough have some wash, as this will help bind them to the scones.

Bake in the oven for 13–17 minutes, depending on the size of your scones. Once done, the tops will be golden brown and well risen. Perfect with jam and clotted cream, or crush fresh raspberries for the little ones.

# Sweet Raisin Scones

## Ingredients

Ingredients as on page 122, plus:

80g (½ cup) sultanas

### From the pantry

1 heaped tbsp caster sugar (superfine)

1 tsp vanilla extract

Follow method as on the left, but add the caster sugar and raisins to the flour and the vanilla extract to the milk, egg and oil bowl before combining (pictured on page 124, top).

# Curried Cheese Scones

## Ingredients

Ingredients as on page 122, plus:

100g (3½oz) Cheddar cheese*, coarsely grated

### From the pantry

1 heaped tsp mild curry powder

freshly ground black pepper

Add the Cheddar, curry powder and a little black pepper to the flour and stir before continuing as per the recipe above (pictured on page 125).

 *Love your leftovers*

Store all scones in an airtight container at room temperature for 3-4 days, or freeze for up to 3 months. Defrost thoroughly before reheating in a warm oven at 170°C fan (190°C/375°F/Gas 5) for 4–5 minutes to refresh.

Sweet Raisin and
Butter-free Scones
(see pages 122–123)

Curried Cheese Scones (see pages 122–123), Cauli and Broccoli Cheese Soup (see page 181)

# What's for dinner?

# Moroccan Couscous Chicken Bake

Comforting and warming, this bake uses couscous as a delicious cheap alternative to traditional pasta.

 **Serves 2 adults and 2-3 littles**

 **Prep 5 mins, Bake 45-55 mins**

## Ingredients

250g (1½ cups) dried couscous

6 skin-on chicken thighs

### From the pantry

2 x 400g (15oz) cans of chickpeas in water

2 tsp ground cumin

3 tsp smoked or unsmoked paprika

2 tsp garlic granules

500g (1lb 2oz) tomato passata (strained tomatoes)

sunflower oil

salt and freshly ground black pepper

Preheat the oven to 200°C fan (220°C/425°F/Gas 7) and find a high-sided oven dish large enough to hold the chicken thighs without overlapping.

Rinse the chickpeas in a strainer under cold running water, then add to the baking dish. Now add the spices and a good grinding of black pepper. Use a spoon to stir the chickpeas and coat in all the spices, this helps them to distribute evenly and removes any clumps. Now add the passata, and swill the empty carton with around 400ml (1⅔ cups) of cold water, to get as much of the excess tomato as possible. Add this to the tray along with the couscous, then give it all a final stir.

Add the chicken thighs on top, skin-side up. If you're lazy like me, arrange them so any excess skin lies over the side of the dish, this will help it crisp up. Alternatively, you can cut them off before adding to the dish, just try to avoid too much skin sitting in the centre of the dish submerged in the sauce, as this will go soggy and is not too nice to eat.

Add a drizzle of oil to each piece of chicken, then season with a little salt and pepper, you can avoid seasoning the chicken portion designated for your little ones. Now place the dish in the centre of the oven and bake for 45–55 minutes, or until the chicken is golden on top, super crispy and cooked throughout. The sauce should have soaked up into the couscous now too. Leave to stand for a few minutes to allow the couscous to settle and the chicken to rest.

**Note** When serving to little ones under 2, standard chickpeas are too small to be a choking hazard, but on occasions you can get large ones which pose more of a risk.

 **Love your leftovers**

This dish will keep in the fridge for 2 days, add a splash more water, and place back in the oven at 180°C fan (200°C/400°F/Gas 6) for 20 minutes or until the chicken is piping hot throughout again. You can also freeze leftovers for up to 3 months, thaw completely before reheating as above.

When serving to little ones under 2, mash their portion of couscous slightly with the back of a fork to break down the chickpeas slightly. Remove the chicken from the bone and serve in finger strips.

# Chinese Steamed Rice Meatballs

Soft meat, coated in rice and steamed until tender is the perfect finger food for little ones, and utterly glorious dipped in chilli oil for us grown-ups.

GF

EF

DF*

V*

Vg*

**Makes
10 balls**

**Prep 7 mins,
Cook 25 mins**

## Ingredients

300g (10½oz) minced (ground) lean pork or plant-based mince*

3 spring onions (scallions), finely diced

**From the pantry**

100g (generous ½ cup) long-grain rice

1 small egg*

1 tsp sesame oil (optional)

2 tbsp low-salt soy sauce*

1 low-salt chicken or vegetable stock cube*

3–5 tbsp cornflour (cornstarch)

2 garlic cloves, crushed

Place the rice in a bowl and cover with cold water. Leave to stand for 1 hour or so, overnight is also great. If you forget, don't worry, this dish will still be delicious, with the rice having a little bit more of a chew once cooked.

When ready to cook, drain the rice and place back into the bowl, ready for rolling. Set your steamer baskets ready for filling on the work surface, preferably use metal vegetable steamer pans, or you can use bamboo ones too. If using bamboo, line each basket with non-stick baking paper, cutting a few holes to allow the steam to get through.

Now, to make the balls, to a bowl, add the minced pork, egg, spring onions, sesame oil, if using, soy sauce, crumbled stock cube and 3 tablespoons of the cornflour. Give it a really good stir; if the mixture feels too wet, add another tablespoon or two of the cornflour, ensuring not to overmix the mixture. It will still be a rather wet mixture, but you should be able to mould it roughly into balls. Do this with clean hands, wetting them will stop the mixture sticking to your hands too much. Take a walnut-sized amount of the meat mixture, roughly roll into a ball, then drop into the uncooked rice, rolling all around so the rice sticks to the raw meat. Place the rice meatball into the steamer basket and repeat with the remaining mixture. Ensure the balls are not touching and spaced apart to allow the steam to cook them evenly.

Once all rolled, allow a pan of water to come to the boil, then place the steamer baskets on top with the lid on, and steam for 25 minutes. Once done, leave the lid on, but turn off the heat and allow to rest for 5 minutes.

Sprinkle over some more spring onion and sesame seeds if you wish, to serve. Fantastic with chilli oil or soy sauce for dipping. For little ones, either serve whole, or cut in half if it's easier for them to pick up independently.

## Love your leftovers

Store for 24 hours, reheat in the steamer or microwave until piping hot throughout. Freeze for 1 month; defrost fully before reheating.

If serving to older children and adults, add a good dollop of mango chutney to the meat sauce when cooking to add more sweetness and flavour.

# Babotie

The national dish of South Africa, this sweet and rich meat dish, flavoured with curry and a custard-like topping is a great one for colder days, or enjoy slightly cooled with a little side salad in the spring.

**Serves 2 adults and 3 littles**

**Prep 20 mins, Bake 30-40 mins**

## Ingredients

300g (10½oz) frozen veg mix (onion, carrot and celery)

500g (1lb 2oz) 5% fat minced (ground) beef

2 slices of stale bread*

70g (2½oz) seedless raisins

### From the pantry

oil, for frying

3 tsp mild curry powder

2 garlic cloves, minced

1 low-salt beef stock cube*

1 tsp mixed dried herbs

approx. 280ml (1¼ cups) milk*

3 eggs

freshly ground black pepper

Preheat the oven to 180°C fan (200°C/400°F/Gas 6).

To a large frying pan or ceramic ovenproof shallow-sided dish, add the oil and place over a medium-high heat. Once hot, add the veg mix and sauté until softened and completely defrosted. Then add the meat and curry powder and cook until the meat has browned, breaking the meat up with a wooden spoon so there's no large clumps.

Add the garlic, crumble in the stock cube, add the dried herbs and a generous grinding of black pepper and stir well. Then top up with 300ml (1¼ cups) of boiling water from the kettle and stir again.

While that comes up to a boil, add 50ml (scant ¼ cup) of milk to a measuring jug, and break up the bread roughly, adding it to the milk. Soak very well and set aside for a moment.

Measure the raisins onto a chopping board and, using a large sharp knife, run the blade over the raisins a few times to cut them in half or into little pieces, there's no need to be precise, we just want to chop them up a little. Then add them to the mince which should now be boiling. Cook for a few minutes, stirring often.

Then take the bread and, with clean hands, squeeze out most of the milk and add the bread to the meat sauce. Stir vigorously to mash the bread into the sauce and leave to boil for a few minutes while you make the topping.

**Recipe continues on page 134**

To the bowl with the leftover bread-soaking milk, top up to reach 230ml (1 cup) of milk, then add the eggs and whisk very well.

Now either pour the meat mixture into an ovenproof casserole dish, or use the pan the mince was cooked in if it can go in the oven.

Level out the meat sauce, then gently and slowly pour the milky eggs over the top. Pour it close to the meat so that it sits on top, rather than seeping down inside the sauce, which it may do if poured from a height.

Carefully place the dish in the centre of the oven and bake for 30–40 minutes until the top is set and golden. Allow to stand for 5 minutes before serving.

Adults, add a little salt to your portion and traditionally this dish has a little spicy heat, so feel free to add some chilli flakes to your portion.

· · · · · · · · · · · · · · · · · · · · · · · · · · · · · · · · · · · · · · · · · · · · · · · · · · · · · · · · · · · · · · · · · ·

 *Love your leftovers*

Leftovers will store in the fridge for 2 days, reheat in the oven for 15 minutes or microwave for 2–3 minutes, stirring halfway through. You can also freeze portions of this for up to 2 months, defrost thoroughly in the fridge and reheat as above.

# Fajita Lasagne

GF*

EF

DF*

A mash-up of two of my favourite dinners – lasagne and fajitas. Cumin-spiced meat sauce layered with tortilla wraps instead of pasta and topped with a traditional cheese sauce, yum!

**Serves 3 adults and 3 littles**

**Prep 20 mins, Bake 20-25 mins**

## Ingredients

400g (14oz) minced (ground) lean beef

1 medium onion

1 red pepper

1 orange pepper

80g (2¾oz) Cheddar cheese*, grated

6 mini tortilla wraps*

### From the pantry

1 tsp ground cumin

2 tsp smoked paprika

1 low-salt beef stock cube*

500g (1lb 2oz) passata (strained tomatoes)

550ml (2½ cups) milk*

50g (scant ¼ cup) unsalted butter*

40g (scant ⅓ cup) cornflour (cornstarch)

freshly ground black pepper

Preheat the oven to 180°C fan (200°C/400°F/Gas 6).

To a large frying pan set over a high heat, add the beef and break up using a wooden spoon. Cook for 4 minutes until browned.

Meanwhile, dice the onion and add this to the mince too. Core and cut the peppers into short strips and set aside.

Back to the beef, add the cumin, smoked paprika, crumbled stock cube and a generous grinding of black pepper. Stir and toss to coat the meat in all the flavours, then add the passata. Stir well and turn the heat down to low. Simmer for 10 minutes.

While the meat sauce cooks, quickly whip up the cheese sauce. Measure the milk into a jug and microwave on HIGH for 2 minutes.

Meanwhile, add the butter to a non-stick pan over a high heat, melt for 30 seconds, then add the cornflour. Stir and cook for 1–2 minutes before gradually pouring in the warmed milk, whisking continuously.

Between each dash of milk added, whisk very well to ensure all the lumps have been removed. Once all the milk has been added you should have a thick and smooth white sauce. Turn off the heat and add the cheese, reserving a little for on top.

**Recipe continues on page 136**

Mix the peppers into the meat sauce, turning off the heat, ready to assemble the lasagne. To a medium ovenproof dish, add one third of the beef mixture. Then add a couple of spoonfuls of the white sauce, spreading out over the top.

Add two tortillas, if they overlap a little, tear this section off and patch up any exposed areas if you wish. Then add more meat, more cheese sauce, and again another two tortillas.

Finally, add the remaining third of the beef sauce, the last two tortillas, and this time liberally top the entire dish with lots of cheese sauce, evening out and pushing some into any of the edges that need to be filled.

Sprinkle over the remaining cheese, add some black pepper and bake for 20–25 minutes until golden on top. Allow to stand for 5–10 minutes before serving with a side salad and guacamole if you wish. Adults, this one is delicious with some hot sauce on your portion.

 *Love your leftovers*

Leftovers will store covered in the fridge for 2 days or freeze for up to 3 months. Defrost thoroughly before reheating in an oven preheated to 200°C fan (220°C/425°F/Gas 7) for 15 minutes, or until piping hot throughout.

You can swap the minced beef for chicken strips, cooking for 5 minutes before adding the other ingredients. Opt for a chicken stock cube if you wish. To make it veggie, use canned beans in the tomato sauce.

**Savoury Chicken Crumble** (see pages 140–141)

# Savoury Chicken Crumble

Gloriously comforting, this dish is a savoury take on the classic sweet treat we all love and a great way to make a small amount of meat stretch further. Tender chicken in a creamy pea sauce, topped with crunchy crumble, delicious! A hug in a bowl.

 **Serves 4 adults and 2 littles**

 **Prep 20 mins, Bake 30-35 mins**

## Ingredients

400g (14oz) diced chicken

300g (10½oz) frozen peas

100g (3½oz) Cheddar cheese*, grated

### From the pantry

40g (2½ tbsp) cornflour (cornstarch), plus 2 tbsp

1 tbsp oil

1 tsp mixed dried herbs

1 low-salt chicken stock cube*

200g plain (all-purpose) flour*

mixed seeds for topping (optional)

freshly ground black pepper

650ml (2¾ cups) milk*

110g (scant ½ cup) unsalted butter*

Preheat the oven to 180°C fan (200°C/400°F/Gas 6).

Coat the chicken in 2 tablespoons of cornflour, stirring to cover every surface. Heat a large heavy-based frying pan and add the oil. Add the chicken in an even layer and cook for 5 minutes until browned on all sides. It doesn't need to be cooked through at this point.

Meanwhile, prep the sauce by measuring the 40g (2½ tablespoons) of cornflour into a jug, then adding the milk, starting with 50ml (scant ¼ cup) and stirring well until the cornflour has dissolved. Stir continuously while you add the remaining milk to avoid it clumping. Set aside until you need it.

Once the chicken has browned, add 10g (scant 1 tablespoon) of butter and while it melts, add the mixed dried herbs, crumbled stock cube and a good grinding of black pepper, keeping the pan over a high heat.

Once the butter has melted, stir the jug of milk and cornflour into the chicken in one go, using a spatula. It should start to thicken instantly on the edges. Now add the frozen peas, stir well and leave to simmer for 5 minutes, stirring often until the sauce has thickened. If you feel it is far too thick, add a dash more milk to loosen.

While the sauce thickens, make your crumble topping. To a mixing bowl, measure in the flour, add a good grinding of black pepper, then add the cold butter in cubes. Using the tips of your fingers, rub the flour into the butter until it resembles rough breadcrumbs. Leave a good few pea-sized pieces of butter as this will create lots of crispy bits.

Once the sauce has thickened, pour the entire contents of the pan into an ovenproof dish (if your frying pan is oven-safe you can keep it in this). Sprinkle over the cheese in an even layer, then scatter the crumble topping over the top. I like to add a little more grated cheese around the edges as this will go deliciously crispy.

Scatter over the seeds, if using (pumpkin and sunflower seeds are my favourite here), then bake for 30–35 minutes until bubbling at the edges and golden on top.

Leave to stand for 5 minutes before serving. For little ones under 2, avoid offering large seeds, or scoop up using a spoon and run a knife over to make them a smaller, safer size. They add a delicious nutty taste to the dish and a great source of fibre and nutrients, so good to offer if you can.

**Veggie swaps –** Replace the chicken for 300g (10½oz) button mushrooms.

This is a great one to make ahead as you can prep the sauce and pour into the pie dish to cool. Make the topping and keep separately in the fridge. Once ready to bake, add the toppings and bake as above.

 **Love your leftovers**

Leftovers will keep for 3 days in the fridge, or freeze for up to 3 months. Defrost thoroughly before reheating in an oven preheated to 200°C fan (220°C/425°F/Gas 7) for 20–25 minutes until piping hot throughout.

# Saag Macaroni Chicken Bake

 GF*

 EF

DF

The combination of lightly spiced curry pasta, which has been cooked in those umami chicken juices, paired with nutritious spinach which just kinda melts into the dish is utter heaven. I could eat this 7 days a week!

 **Serves 2 adults and 2 littles**

 **Prep 7 mins, Bake 40-50 mins**

## Ingredients

6–7 blocks of frozen chopped spinach

300g (10½oz) macaroni*

600–700g (1lb 5oz–1lb 9oz) skin-on chicken legs or thighs

### From the pantry

2 low-salt chicken stock cubes*

1 tbsp garlic granules

1–2 heaped tbsp mild curry powder

sunflower or garlic oil

salt and freshly ground black pepper

Preheat the oven to 200°C fan (220°C/425°F/Gas 7), and boil the kettle. To a large, high-sided ovenproof dish, crumble in the stock cubes and add the spinach. Grind in a generous amount of black pepper, and add the garlic granules and curry powder. Now measure 800ml (3⅔ cups) of boiling water from the kettle into a heatproof jug and quickly add to the tray. Stir well and allow to stand for 3–4 minutes, giving the spinach cubes a bit of a poke with a spoon every now and then to help the outsides melt.

The spinach cubes don't need to be completely melted, but the outsides will now have become softer and some of the spinach pieces will be floating in the water. Add the pasta and stir really well before laying the chicken pieces on top, skin-side up. Cover the dish tightly with foil, then place in the centre of the oven.

After 20 minutes, remove the foil, and give the pasta in between the chicken pieces a little stir. The spinach blocks will have dissolved now, so if you see any big clusters, gently mix these in, and then push down any pieces of pasta that are sticking up as these will catch easily. Drizzle a little oil over the top of the entire dish, and season the chicken skin with salt and pepper if you wish. Remember little ones don't need to eat the salty skin, just the soft meat underneath. If you wish, you can also grab a pinch of curry powder and scatter over the top of the dish for an extra hit of flavour. Now pop the dish back in the oven, uncovered this time, and bake for a further 20–30 minutes until the chicken is crispy and the pasta is cooked through.

 **Love your leftovers**

Any leftovers will keep for up to 2 days covered in the fridge. Transfer the pasta to a smaller ovenproof dish, which will fit the contents snugly, then add the chicken on top before you store. When you come to reheat, add a splash of water to the pasta underneath, drizzle the top with a little oil and bake at 200°C fan (220°C/425°F/Gas 7) for 20–30 minutes until the chicken is piping hot throughout. You can also freeze the leftovers, thawing completely before reheating as above.

# Courgette and Chicken Meatballs

You can use turkey mince here too, whichever takes your fancy or comes up cheaper. With courgette added these meatballs are super moist and succulent, perfect as a snack, part of a meal or great to batch cook for days ahead.

 **Makes 16**

 **Prep 10 mins, Cook 10-25 mins**

## Ingredients

500g (1lb 2oz) minced (ground) chicken

60g (2oz) Parmesan or Cheddar*, finely grated

1 medium courgette

### From the pantry

1 egg

1 tsp garlic mince or purée

70g (2½oz) breadcrumbs*

1 tbsp cornflour (cornstarch)

1 tbsp oil

freshly ground black pepper

### For the sauce

500g (1lb 2oz) passata (strained tomatoes)

2 tsp smoked paprika

1 tsp dried mixed herbs

1 tsp sugar (optional)

freshly ground black pepper

To a bowl, add the chicken mince, finely grated cheese, egg, garlic, breadcrumbs, cornflour and black pepper. Now grate the courgette and, over the sink, either in sections or all together wrapped in a tea towel, squeeze the courgette to remove all the excess moisture. Add the pulp to the bowl too.

You can cook these meatballs in the oven, air fryer or frying pan. If cooking in the oven, set a large lined baking tray in front of you ready to put the meatballs on. If cooking in the air fryer, have the basket in front of you and a plate for round 2 of cooking. Or if frying in a pan, a plate to place the meatballs on.

Now, with clean hands, squish the chicken mixture together, so that all the ingredients are really well combined. Then one at a time, roll into 16 golfball-sized meatballs, placing on your chosen vessel as you go.

Drizzle with the oil and ensure the balls are not touching. Bake in the oven at 200°C fan (220°C/425°F/Gas 7) for 20–25 minutes, air-fry at 200°C (400°F) for 15 minutes, or pan-fry over a medium-high heat for 10–12 minutes, turning often to brown on all sides.

Allow to rest for a few minutes before serving in your favourite way. We like to dip ours into a quick and easy tomato sauce (see below), this also works perfectly to make pasta and chicken meatballs too (as pictured on this book's cover!).

## Quick tomato sauce

Add all the ingredients to a saucepan and simmer until piping hot. This consistency is great for pasta sauces, or you can allow the sauce to simmer for 5–10 minutes to thicken to your desired consistency.

 **Love your leftovers**

Leftovers will store in an airtight container for 3 days in the fridge or for up to 3 months in the freezer. Defrost thoroughly, then reheat in a hot oven for 10 minutes or air fryer for 6–8 minutes until piping hot.

If you'd like to hide the courgettes in the finished dish, peel the skin off before grating to disguise the green edges.

# One-pan Pea and Chicken Bake

The humble frozen pea has its moment to shine in this dish. Convenient, cheap, nutritious and utterly delicious, this dish was a real winner with my Nina.

 **Serves 2 adults and 3 littles**

**Prep 5 mins, Bake 40-45 mins**

## Ingredients

600g (1lb 5oz) frozen peas

6–8 skin-on chicken pieces

### From the pantry

2 heaped tbsp cornflour (cornstarch)

2 tsp garlic granules

1 low-salt chicken stock cube*

½ tsp mixed dried herbs

2 tbsp low-salt soy sauce*

salt and freshly ground black pepper (optional)

Preheat the oven to 200°C fan (220°C/425°F/Gas 7).

To a large, high-sided ovenproof dish, add the frozen peas. Spoon in the cornflour and stir really well to coat the peas in the flour, this helps distribute the flour evenly, avoiding clumps. Now add the garlic granules, crumbled stock cube and dried herbs. Mix again, before adding just enough cold water to cover the peas, don't add too much as the dish will become very liquid when cooked. Add the soy sauce, then stir it all really well.

Lay the chicken on top, skin-side up, ensuring any excess skin hangs over the edge of your dish rather than submerged in the liquid, as this will result in limp floppy chicken skin rather than crispiness. Season the skin if you wish too, which will help it crisp up even more.

Place the dish in the centre of the oven and bake uncovered for 40–45 minutes, or until the chicken has cooked through.

Serve with boiled potatoes, mash, pasta or simply in a bowl with some buttered bread for dipping, delicious.

 **Love your leftovers**

Leftovers will keep in the fridge for 2 days, simply place back into an ovenproof dish, and bake until the chicken is piping hot and crisp again. You can also freeze this for up to 3 months, thawing completely before reheating as above.

Any cut of chicken will work here, such as chunks of breast or boneless thigh, but bone-in gives that bit of extra flavour.

# Comforting Chicken and Dumplings

A thick rich sauce, filled with veggies, succulent chicken, and light dumplings, this is the perfect dish to make when your family need a big hug on a cold day. And the best thing is that this dish makes two meals, because if you have any leftovers, it makes the most delicious pie (see Love your leftovers page 150).

*2 adults and
2 littles*

*Prep 15 mins,
Cook 35 mins*

## Ingredients

5 bone-in chicken thighs

300g (10½oz) frozen veg base mix (celery, carrot, onion)

300g (10½oz) frozen peas

### From the pantry

5 tbsp sunflower or olive oil

650ml (2¾ cups) milk* or replace with water

200g (1½ cups), plus 3 tbsp plain (all-purpose) flour*

3 tsp mixed herbs

2 low-salt chicken stock cubes*

2 tsp baking powder*

freshly ground black pepper

To a large, lidded saucepan, add 2 tablespoons of oil and set over a high heat.

While that comes up to temperature, remove the skin from the chicken thighs, then add to the hot pan in an even layer. Cook for 3 minutes to brown, then flip and cook for a further 3 minutes.

Once the outside has browned, but the inside is still raw, remove the chicken and set aside in a bowl.

Now add the frozen veg mix (not the peas) and allow to sauté in the chicken juices for 4 minutes. Use a wooden spoon to scrape the bottom of the pan to lift up any caramelized pieces of chicken, this is where all the flavour is. Once the veggies are soft and fully defrosted, add 3 tablespoons of the flour and stir well.

Measure 500ml (generous 2 cups) of milk into a jug, then after a few minutes of stirring the flour into the veggies to help the flour taste cook out, gradually pour in the milk, stirring continuously to avoid it clumping and to lift any crispy bits from the base of the pan.

While you wait for the milk to come to the boil, add a good grinding of black pepper, 2 teaspoons of mixed dried herbs, and crumble in the stock cubes.

Then add the chicken and any resting juices. Pour in enough boiling water from the kettle to completely submerge the chicken so the liquid level sits approx. 2.5cm (1in) above it. Turn the heat down to low and put a lid on the pan while you make the dumplings.

**Recipe continues on page 150**

To make the dumplings, add the flour, 1 teaspoon of mixed herbs, baking powder and a little more black pepper to the bowl you set the chicken aside in (to save on washing up).

Stir well, then add 3 tablespoons of oil and 150ml (⅔ cup) of milk. Mix to combine but try not to overmix as this will result in a dense dumpling.

Take the lid off the pan, then using two tablespoons, drop tablespoon amounts of the batter into the stew, using one spoon to scrape the dumpling batter off the other spoon.

Stir gently to submerge the dumplings, then put the lid on and cook for 20 minutes. Refrain from lifting the lid to take a peek as your dumplings won't rise as well.

After 20 minutes, lift the lid, stir gently and add the frozen peas, stir again, then pop the lid back on and cook for a further 3 minutes.

For little ones, remove the chicken from the bone-in strips, and cut the dumplings in half. Adults, you may wish to add some salt to your portion.

 *Love your leftovers*

Leftovers will last in the fridge in an airtight container for 3 days or freeze for up to 3 months. Defrost thoroughly before bringing up to a rolling boil for at least 5 minutes in a saucepan until the chicken is piping hot throughout. If you'd like to make a pie from the leftover stew, remove the chicken from the bone and chop into chunks along with any leftover dumplings. Pour into an oven dish, top with puff pastry, egg wash and bake at 200°C fan (220°C/425°F/Gas 7) for 20 minutes until puffed up and golden.

# Cumberland Pie

A take on the classic cottage pie; traditional Cumberland Pie would use beef pieces, which you slow cook to soften. My cheaper and quicker version uses minced beef instead and it's just as delicious. You can keep it classic with crispy sliced potatoes on top like mine or opt for mash instead if you fancy.

**Serves 3 adults and 3 littles**

**Prep 20 mins, Bake 25 mins**

## Ingredients

5 medium all-rounder potatoes

500g (1lb 2oz) minced (ground) beef

300g (10½oz) frozen classic chopped vegetables (celery, onion, carrot)

2 handfuls of grated Cheddar cheese*

**From the pantry**

2 low-salt beef stock cubes*

2 tsp mixed dried herbs

2 garlic cloves, crushed, or 1 tsp garlic granules

500g (1lb 2oz) passata (strained tomatoes)

2 tbsp Worcestershire sauce* (optional)

5 tbsp breadcrumbs*

2 tbsp oil of choice

freshly ground black pepper

---

Preheat the oven to 180°C fan (200°C/400°F/Gas 6).

Boil the kettle and meanwhile peel the potatoes, leaving them whole. Add to a pan along with the boiled water, set the pan over a high heat and allow to come up to a rolling boil. Cook for 15–20 minutes until the spuds are tender when a knife is inserted.

While the potatoes cook, make the filling. Add the beef to an ovenproof, shallow-sided casserole dish. If you don't have one of these, make the filling in a medium saucepan and transfer to an oven dish to assemble.

Brown the mince until you see no raw meat. Ideally use lean steak mince, but if your mince has a higher fat ratio, spoon some of the excess fat into a bowl to discard.

Now add the frozen veg mix, or you can use fresh and chop up finely into small cubes yourself. Cook with the mince until it has heated up and is starting to soften.

Crumble in the stock cubes, add the dried herbs, garlic and a good grinding of black pepper. Stir well, then add the passata. Swill out the empty carton with cold water (approx. 150ml/⅔ cup) and add this to the mince too. If you have a bottle in the cupboard, add the Worcestershire sauce, then give everything a really good stir. Put the lid on and simmer for 15 minutes, stirring every so often.

**Recipe continues on page 152**

Once the potatoes are tender, drain away the hot water and fill the pan up with cold water from the tap, drain this away too and fill up again with more cold water. This will rapidly cool down the potatoes, making them easier to handle.

Slice the potatoes as thinly as you can, ideally around 5mm (¼in) in thickness. I find it easier to use the bridge method, slicing the potato as a whole and keeping it together the whole time, as the inside will still be very hot and you run the risk of scalding yourself if you hold the cut insides.

Now, to assemble, either pour the mince into a medium ceramic oven dish, or if your mince pan is ovenproof keep it in there. Layer the sliced potato over the top of the mince, only overlap a little at the edges. Scatter over the grated cheese and breadcrumbs, then drizzle over the oil to help the top crisp up well.

Bake for 25–30 minutes until golden and bubbling at the edges. Allow the dish to sit for 5 minutes before tucking in.

Serve as is, or with some extra veggies on the side. For little ones, cut the potatoes into finger strips so it's easier to hold them, or gently crush the spuds into the mince to make a lumpy mash.

· · · · · · · · · · · · · · · · · · · · · · · · · · · · · · · · · · · · · · · · · · · · · · · · · · · · · · · · · · · · · · · · · · · · · · · · · · · · · · · · · · · · · · · · · · · · · · · · · · · · · · ·

 *Love your leftovers*

Leftovers will keep in the fridge for 2 days or freeze for up to 3 months. Allow to defrost thoroughly before reheating in the oven at 200°C fan (220°C/425°F/Gas 7) for 20 minutes until it is piping hot throughout.

# Vegetarian

# No-cook Satay Noodle Salad

This cold dish is perfect to whip up for picnics or light lunches on those warmer summer days. There's no cooking involved, so this is the ultimate fuss-free meal, plus it's a great way to get in those essential nutrients found in nut butter.

***Serves 1 adult and 1 little***

***5-10 mins***

## Ingredients

70g (2½oz) thin rice noodles

60g (¼ cup) smooth or crunchy peanut butter (100% nuts)

80g (2¾oz) carrot, peeled

100g (3½oz) cucumber

### From the pantry

1 tsp garlic purée, or 1 small garlic clove, crushed

1 tsp sesame oil (optional)

2 tbsp low-salt soy sauce*

Add the noodles to a bowl and cover with boiling water. Allow to soak according to the packet instructions, usually between 3–5 minutes. Stir with a fork after 1 minute to break up the noodles so they soften consistently.

Meanwhile, make the sauce. Add the peanut butter, garlic, sesame oil, if you have it, and soy sauce to a salad bowl. Add 2 tablespoons of the hot water your noodles are steeping in, then mix the sauce really well. It will initially look like the peanut butter has split but keep stirring and it'll turn into a loose, creamy sauce.

Now coarsely grate the veggies and add that to the peanut sauce. By now the noodles should be soft, taste one to double check before straining and rinsing under a cold tap. Shake off the excess water before chopping the noodles into small pieces, approx. 1–2cm (½–¾in) in length. I like to do this with scissors in a bowl, or you can use a knife on a chopping board.

Add the chopped noodles to the satay sauce and salad, then give it a really good stir and serve. This one will be a little messy for little ones to enjoy independently but a great way for them to taste these different flavours, so I say embrace the mess if you can! Allow baby to practise using a child-friendly fork, with some preloading help from yourself.

 ***Love your leftovers***

Leftovers will keep in the fridge for 2 days, stir again before serving. Not suitable for home freezing.

# Baked Coconut Lentil Rice

Make use of the oven being on by cooking the rice in the oven too, a great side dish to have alongside some veggies and meat of your choice. We love it with wings or baked fish.

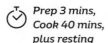

**2 adults and 3 little as a side**

**Prep 3 mins, Cook 40 mins, plus resting**

## Ingredients

1 x 400g (14oz) can of coconut milk

235g (8½ oz) drained canned green lentils (in unsalted water)

### From the pantry

250g (1⅓ cups) white long-grain or basmati rice

1 vegetable stock cube*

2 garlic cloves

3 heaped tsp mild curry powder

Preheat the oven to 180°C fan (200°C/400°F/Gas 6).

Crumble the stock cube into a large ceramic baking dish. Measure 250ml (generous 1 cup) of boiling water and add to the dish, allowing the stock cube to dissolve. Crush or grate in the garlic cloves and add the curry powder. Now pour in the coconut milk and stir a little.

Wash the rice until the water runs clear, then add the lentils to the strainer, rinsing the lentils over the rice. Shake to remove most of the excess water, then add the rice and lentils to the baking dish. Stir really well and level out the rice and lentils under the liquid. If you're serving to older kiddos, salt the dish now, alternatively, adults you can salt your portion once cooked if you wish.

Cover the dish tightly with foil and bake for 40 minutes. Remove from the oven, keep the foil on and allow to stand for 5–10 minutes. All the water should be evaporated now, so you can fluff up the rice with a fork and serve.

**To cook on the hob** Wash the rice and set aside with the lentils. Add a drizzle of oil to a large saucepan over a medium-high heat and sauté the garlic and spices for 30 seconds. Add the rice and lentils and cook for a further 30 seconds before adding the coconut milk, boiling water and crumbled stock cube. Stir well and put the lid on. Allow to come to a simmer, then turn the heat to low and cook for 11 minutes. Don't remove the lid in this time. Allow to stand for a further 2 minutes with the lid on before fluffing with a fork and serving.

### Love your leftovers

Leftovers must be cooled within an hour and refrigerated as soon as possible. Consume within 24 hours to keep it safe to eat. Alternatively, freeze for up to 2 months. I find it best to reheat rice in the microwave, in a covered microwaveable bowl. Reheat for 30–60 seconds from fresh, or 2–3 minutes from frozen.

You could add a handful of grated courgette or carrot to the dish, plus some extra chunks of meat or plant-based protein, for a one-pot dinner to cook all together.

# Curried Rösti Pasties

With no parboiling of the spuds, this quick to whip up recipe is comforting and a real celebration of the humble potato!

 GF*

 EF*

 DF*

V

Vg*

 **Makes 4**

 **Prep 10 mins, Bake 25-30 mins**

## Ingredients

350g (12oz) all-rounder white potatoes

80g (2¾oz) Cheddar cheese*, grated

1 x 320g (11oz) puff pastry sheet*

### From the pantry

1 heaped tsp mild curry powder

2 tsp garlic granules

freshly ground black pepper

1 egg or milk* to wash

Preheat the oven to 180°C fan (200°C/400°F/Gas 6) and line a large baking tray.

Peel the potatoes then grate on the fine side of a box grater. Then either add to a clean tea towel and squeeze over the sink to remove the moisture, or take small sections in your hands and squeeze out the excess starch over a bowl. It doesn't need to be bone dry, just not soggy.

Add the potato to a medium mixing bowl, followed by the curry powder, garlic granules and black pepper. Stir well, then add the cheese and stir again, ensuring the cheese is mixed well into the potato. I find using my fingertips easiest for this.

Unroll the puff pastry sheet and cut into 4 rectangles. Crack the egg into a small bowl, whisk, then use a pastry brush to egg wash each piece, trying not to let the egg drip down the sides of the cut edges.

Divide the potato mixture between the pastry rectangles, forming it into a thick line and leaving two opposite corners clean.

Then take one of these corners and fold over the filling. Egg wash the top and fold the other clean corner over and overlap. The egg wash will help it stick and stay together. Repeat with the rest and place onto your prepared baking tray. Egg wash all of the exposed pastry and bake for 25–30 minutes until puffed up and lovely and golden on top.

Serve in finger strips for little ones with a side salad. Adults, add a touch of salt – these are delicious dunked into your favourite mustard, or yogurt for little ones who may prefer a milder taste.

**Note** To add extra veggies in here, swap 100g (3½oz) of the potato for half a large courgette, grated and squeezed too.

**Leftovers** will keep for up to 3 days in the fridge. Reheat in the oven at 180°C fan (200°C/400°F/Gas 6) for 10 mins or air-fry at 180°C (350°F) for 5 mins until piping hot. Freeze for up to 3 months, reheating as above adding 5 mins to the time.

# Sunshine Veg Tart

Simple to whip up, this delicious vegetable pastry slice will be a huge crowd-pleaser.

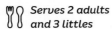 **Serves 2 adults and 3 littles**

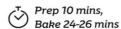 **Prep 10 mins, Bake 24–26 mins**

## Ingredients

100g (3½oz) sweet peppers, preferably mix of colours

6 cherry tomatoes, quartered

1 x 320g (11oz) sheet of ready-rolled puff pastry*

100g (3½oz) cream cheese*

70g (2½oz) Cheddar cheese*

### From the pantry

130g (4½oz) canned sweetcorn in water, drained

1 tbsp mild tandoori spice mix, or mild curry powder

1 tbsp sunflower or garlic-infused oil

freshly ground black pepper

Preheat the oven to 200°C fan (220°C/425°F/Gas 7) and line a large shallow baking sheet with non-stick baking paper.

Prep the veggies by dicing the peppers into 1cm (½in) cubes; I like to use a mix of yellow, orange and red pepper here, but use whatever you have in.

Unravel the pastry and score a box 1cm (½in) in from the edge, making sure to avoid cutting all the way through the pastry. This is your guide to keep all the toppings inside.

Use the back of a tablespoon to spread the cream cheese over the sheet of pastry, reaching all the corners within the border. Then sprinkle over the diced peppers and drained sweetcorn evenly. Pour the curry powder into a tablespoon measure, then evenly sprinkle over the cream cheese and peppers. Try to avoid getting any on the exposed pastry edge as this will catch in the oven.

Now dot the cherry tomatoes in any gaps between the peppers, and using a fine grater, shred the cheese over the pastry, evenly spreading across the entire tart. Lastly, add a grinding of black pepper and drizzle over a little oil, ensuring you get some on the exposed pastry edges too.

Place ion the top shelf of the oven for 24–26 minutes until the cheese has turned golden, the pastry has puffed up and the base is crisp throughout.

Serve with a side salad and a little couscous if you wish. For little ones, cut into finger strips so it's easier for them to hold.

 **Love your leftovers**

Store leftovers in an airtight container in the fridge if keeping for longer than 12 hours, they'll be fine for 2–3 days. Enjoy cold, or reheat in the oven at 180°C fan (200°C/400°F/Gas 6) for 5–6 minutes until piping hot. Freeze for up to 1 month and reheat in the oven for 10–15 minutes until thoroughly piping hot.

# Crispy Korean Green Bean Pancakes

GF*
EF
DF*
V
Vg*

These are so addictive, crispy on the outside, soft on the inside, packed full of veg. Delicious chopped up in a salad, or just on their own with a little dip for dunking.

**Makes 8 pancakes**

**Prep 5 mins, Cook 10 mins**

### Ingredients

100g (3½oz) fresh green beans

### From the pantry

80g (⅔ cup) self-raising flour*

40g (2½ tbsp) cornflour (cornstarch)

1 tbsp low-salt soy sauce*

1 tsp sesame oil

1 tsp garlic granules

80ml (⅓ cup) milk* or water

1 tbsp sunflower oil

First, prepare the beans. I prefer to cut the green beans in half, then take each piece and slice down the middle making two long thin beans. This way they get really soft when cooking. But it is also delicious if you cut the beans into 5mm (¼in) rounds as if you were finely slicing a spring onion (scallion).

To a bowl, add the flour, cornflour, soy sauce, sesame oil and garlic granules. Then pour in the milk or water and stir to form a thick batter. Add the beans and coat very well in the batter.

Heat a heavy-based non-stick large frying pan over a high heat and add the tablespoon of oil. Once hot, add a heaped tablespoon of the batter and gently spread into a small circle. Don't add too much as the beans won't soften evenly. You'll need to cook these in batches, stick to 4 to give enough room for each pancake to spread. Turn the heat down to medium to avoid burning the outside, then after 1 minute, use a thin plastic spatula to get under each pancake and flip. It may not be golden yet and still quite pale but that's fine for now. Once flipped, apply pressure on the pancake using the back of your spatula, pressing down so that the beans push together and closer to the base of the pan.

Cook the pancakes for 3–4 minutes, pressing often so they get nice and crispy, then flip again and cook for a further minute on the other side to get more colour, pressing again to help them along. You want a crispy outside and a nice golden colour, so keep cooking or turn the heat up if you feel they need a little longer.

Transfer to a plate lined with kitchen paper and repeat with the rest of the batter. You may need to add a touch more oil to the pan for this batch.

 **Love your leftovers**

If you have any left, these will keep in the fridge for 3 days in an airtight container. They can be eaten cold or reheated in a frying pan. You can also freeze for up to 3 months between non-stick baking paper to avoid sticking. Defrost either in the microwave, toaster or at room temperature.

To serve to little ones, cut each pancake in half or into finger strips and serve with a little yogurt for dipping. For us adults, I love these with a little mayo and hot sauce mixed together.

# Lentil Butternut Squash Roast

Looking for a vegetarian alternative for a Sunday roast or accompaniment to a celebration meal? Well, this one is a real winner!

**Makes 6 generous slices**

**Prep 20 mins, Cook 25-30 mins**

## Ingredients

400g (14oz) peeled, deseeded butternut squash

500g (1lb 2oz) canned green lentils

100g (generous 2 cups) dried breadcrumbs*

80g (2¾oz) Cheddar cheese*, grated

### From the pantry

1 tbsp oil, preferably garlic-infused

2 tsp garlic granules

1 tsp smoked paprika

1 tsp mixed dried herbs

3 eggs

freshly ground black pepper

Chop the squash into roughly 1.5cm (⅝in) cubes and cook until soft in whichever way you prefer. I like to do this in an air fryer at 200°C (400°F) for 20 minutes, with a little drizzle of oil, tossing halfway through. Roasting on a large baking sheet in the oven at 200°C fan (220°C/425°F/Gas 7) for approx. 25 minutes works well too. You can also steam, boil or microwave the squash until tender but these methods don't have quite as much flavour.

While the squash cooks, preheat the oven to 200°C fan (220°C/425°F/Gas 7) and line a 900g (2lb) loaf tin with non-stick paper.

Rinse the lentils, then add to a large mixing bowl. Use a potato masher to gently mash the lentils a little, leaving plenty still whole. Then add the breadcrumbs and cheese and mix very well. Add the black pepper, garlic granules, paprika and dried herbs and mix again.

Once the squash is tender, add this to the bowl too and mix immediately to help the squash cool a moment. Crack in the eggs and stir one final time until you have a sticky, wet consistency. Tumble the mixture into the prepared loaf tin and press down with the back of a spoon to level out the top. Drizzle over a little oil and pop in the oven to bake for 25–30 minutes until a golden crust has formed on top.

Allow the roast to sit in the tin for 5–10 minutes to firm up before using the paper to remove onto a chopping board to serve up using a serrated knife. Serve in finger strips to little ones alongside your favourite roast sides.

 **Love your leftovers**

Leftovers will keep in an airtight container in the fridge for up to 3 days. You can also freeze in slices. Defrost thoroughly and reheat in the microwave for 4 minutes; or in a dish with a splash of water covered with foil, bake in the oven at 180°C (200°C/400°F/Gas 6) for 15–20 minutes.

If you have some in the cupboard, a handful of finely chopped nuts is a delicious addition to the mixture. If it's Christmas, add a handful of chopped dried cranberries for a festive touch.

You can also prep this lasagne ahead of time and place in the fridge or freezer unbaked, ready to cook later. Cook from frozen for 1 hour, covered for the first 30 minutes, or until piping hot throughout.

# Frugal Mushroom Lasagne

Mushrooms are fantastically cheap, especially when using frozen ones, and paired with store-cupboard ingredients and items you may already have in your fridge, this lasagne is really easy to whip up and a real crowd-pleaser.

**Serves 3 adults and 3 littles**

**Prep 20 mins, Bake 40 mins**

## Ingredients

1 large onion

500g (1lb 2oz) frozen mushrooms

6 blocks of frozen chopped spinach

170g (6oz) Cheddar cheese*

250g (9oz) dried lasagne sheets*

. . . . . . . . . . . . . .

### From the pantry

drizzle of sunflower oil

1 vegetable stock cube*

1 tsp mixed herbs

3 tbsp reduced-salt soy sauce*

50g (scant ¼ cup) unsalted butter*

800ml (3⅓ cups) milk*

60g (scant ½ cup) plain (all-purpose) flour* or cornflour (cornstarch)

2 garlic cloves

freshly ground black pepper

. . . . . . . . . . . . . . . . . . . . . . . .

Preheat the oven to 170°C fan (190°C/375°F/Gas 5).

Finely dice the onion and add to a large, high-sided frying pan with a little oil. Sauté for 3 minutes until starting to turn translucent, then tip in the frozen mushrooms and add a good grinding of black pepper. Stir and cook for a further 2 minutes to help the mushrooms defrost, then crumble in the stock cube and add 100ml (scant ½ cup) of water. Stir and nestle in the frozen spinach cubes. Simmer for 4 minutes.

Now measure the milk into a microwaveable jug and heat on HIGH for 3 minutes to take the cold edge off. And grate the cheese if it's not already done.

Back to the mushrooms, stir and turn the spinach cubes over, crushing down a little with a wooden spoon to help them melt quicker. Add the mixed herbs and soy sauce and simmer for another 4–5 minutes until the spinach has fully defrosted. Once boiling and the spinach has completely melted, remove from the heat. It will be thick but still a little watery too, don't worry we want that. If your little ones aren't keen on mushroom pieces, give the mixture a whizz to chop everything up a little.

While that cooks, make the white sauce. Melt the butter in a large saucepan over a high heat, then add the flour. Stir well and cook for 30 seconds, then with a whisk or wooden spoon in one hand, add just a splash of the warmed milk. Quickly stir so that as it thickens it turns into a paste, you'll need to add a touch more milk quickly, do this again and whisk repeating the process until you have a very thick mixture. Beat it well to remove any lumps, as it's easier to do that now while the mixture is thick, then gradually add the remaining milk, stirring continuously to combine to form a smooth silky consistency. Allow the sauce to come to the boil, stirring frequently, it should thicken very well within a few minutes of boiling. Once done, remove from the heat and stir in 100g (3½oz) of the grated cheese.

**Recipe continues on page 170**

Now we're ready to assemble. You want a medium ovenproof dish, big enough to lay 3 lasagne sheets on each layer. Start with a thin layer of white sauce, then add the pasta sheets, uncooked. This is why we want the mushroom sauce to be a little runny as all the excess liquid will soak up into the pasta in the oven. Now divide the mushroom sauce into thirds in the pan, then add one third onto the dry pasta. Add a few ladles of white sauce, then repeat the process twice more.

Once you get to the last layer of pasta, top with the remaining white sauce in a thick layer over the top, spreading out to the edges. Sprinkle over the remaining cheese and add a little freshly ground black pepper.

Bake the lasagne, uncovered, for 40–45 minutes until the top is golden and crisp. Serve with a little side salad, adults adding some salt to your portion.

 *Love your leftovers*

Leftover cooked lasagne will keep in the fridge for 2 days, covered, or freeze for up to 3 months in portions. Defrost thoroughly, add to a snug-fitting oven dish, add a splash of water, cover and bake for 15–20 minutes until piping hot throughout.

# Glamorgan Sausages

My simplified version of this classic Welsh dish is utterly gorgeous and one that will make even the most reluctant leek eater want to chow down.

 **Makes 8**

**Prep 10 mins,
Cook 6-8 mins**

## Ingredients

200g (7oz) trimmed leeks

1 tsp mustard of choice*

100g (3½oz) Cheddar or Welsh hard cheese, grated*

### From the pantry

flavourless oil, for cooking

2½ thick slices of bread*

1 egg yolk (optional)*

freshly ground black pepper

Trim the leeks, remove the outer tougher leaves and slice down the centre leaving the root still attached. Rinse under running water in the sink with the root side up so any dirt gets washed away.

Shake off the excess water, then roughly chop a few times into smaller pieces and put in your food processor. Whizz until you have very small pieces, this is what makes them easier to enjoy for all. Alternatively, you can finely slice with a knife.

Preheat a large non-stick frying pan, add a small drizzle of oil and tip in the leeks, using a spatula to transfer every little piece from the processor pot. Fry over a medium heat, stirring often until the leeks have softened.

Meanwhile, make the breadcrumbs. Use a piece of kitchen paper to wipe out the processor pot, it doesn't need to be completely clean. Then add two slices of bread. Whizz until you have very fine breadcrumbs, then tip into a large mixing bowl. Now whizz the last half slice of bread and place this onto a small plate and set aside for later.

Now the leeks are soft, use the spatula to scrape them all into the mixing bowl with the large amount of breadcrumbs. Allow to cool for a moment while you add the remaining ingredients. Add your mustard of choice, we like the yellow American mustard here, a little black pepper and the grated cheese. To help the mixture bind, add the egg yolk, discarding the white or using for another recipe. Then mix it all up very well. If you don't have any eggs or can't eat them, this recipe will still work fine but may be a little trickier to shape on the next stage.

**Recipe continues on page 172**

Divide the mixture into 8 portions, then take each one and form into a little sausage shape, pressing the mixture together if it doesn't want to hold. Then tip each sausage into the plate you have set aside with the remaining breadcrumbs, rolling the sausage around to coat it entirely in crumbs.

Now to cook. Use the same frying pan as you did for the leeks, just give it a little wipe down to remove any remaining bits of leek as these will burn in the next step.

Add 2 tablespoons of oil to the pan and warm up over a medium heat. Once hot when hovering your hand over the pan, add the sausages and cook for 6–8 minutes, turning often to brown on all sides. Towards the end of cooking, one at a time turn each sausage on its sides for 5 or so seconds to seal and brown the sausage ends too.

Once golden and crisp, transfer to a plate lined with kitchen paper to soak up any excess oil, and serve. These are great for a light lunch with a little dip and salad on the side, or you can serve with steamed veggies and mash for a hearty winter warming dinner.

 **Love your leftovers**

Leftovers will store in the fridge for 3 days in an airtight container, enjoy hot or cold. Reheat in the air fryer or hot oven for 5–7 minutes until piping hot throughout. You can also freeze these for up to 3 months, defrost thoroughly before reheating.

# Lentil Ragù

Comforting, hearty and packed full of goodness, this recipe makes a big batch, perfect for making today and freezing for another day. You can also add more water when cooking and make this into a delicious soup.

**Serves 4 adults and 3 littles**

**Prep 10 mins, Cook 40 mins**

## Ingredients

2 small onions or 1 large onion

300g (10½oz) green lentils

5 small carrots

### From the pantry

2 tbsp sunflower oil

2 tbsp tomato purée

2 heaped tsp smoked paprika

2 tsp garlic purée or 3 garlic cloves, crushed

1 low-salt vegetable stock cube*

1 tsp mixed dried herbs

freshly ground black pepper

Fill the kettle and boil ready for later.

Finely dice, or I like to grate the onion so there's no "onion bits" as my Nina calls them. Heat a large heavy-based pot over a medium-high heat, add the oil and the onions. Sauté for 3–4 minutes until soft. If you feel they are catching a little, add a splash of water and stir well until evaporated. Then add the tomato purée and cook for another couple of minutes to remove the tangy tomato taste.

While this cooks, wash the lentils then add them to the softened onions and purée, along with the smoked paprika, garlic, crumbled stock cube, dried herbs and black pepper. Measure 1.5 litres of boiling water into a jug or bowl, then add to the lentils. Stir really well and let it come to the boil.

While it does, peel and grate the carrots, then add these to the lentils too. One more stir and turn the heat down to medium-low and cook for 35–40 minutes, stirring often and especially towards the end to avoid sticking once most of the water has soaked up and evaporated.

Once done, the lentils will have softened; taste a little on a spoon, if they feel gritty, cook for another 5–10 minutes. One final step I like to do to make the ragù a little creamier is to mash with a potato masher for 30 seconds. Just squish around a quarter of the lentils.

Serve with pasta, on a jacket potato, in a big bowl with flatbreads, any way you fancy.

## ♡ Love your leftovers

Leftovers will store for 4 days in the fridge or freeze for up to 4 months. Defrost thoroughly and reheat in a saucepan or microwave until piping hot throughout.

If you prefer to conceal the carrots in the finished dish, finely grate them instead.

# Butter Bean Pasta with Garlic Crunchy Sesame Crumbs

GF*
EF
DF*
V
Vg*

Whip up this delicious, creamy butter bean hummus and use it to coat tagliatelle, or any pasta shape you fancy. Sprinkled with these moreish garlicky crumbs, it's heaven!

 **Serves 2 adults and 2 littles**

 **Prep 5 mins, Cook 11 mins**

## Ingredients

2 thick slices of bread*, stale is best

juice of ½ lemon

### From the pantry

200g (7oz) pasta*

2 garlic cloves

30g (2 tbsp) unsalted butter*

1 tbsp garlic-infused olive oil or sunflower oil

1 tsp dried thyme

3 tbsp sesame seeds

2 tsp garlic granules

400g (14oz) can of butter beans in water

1 tbsp sesame oil

freshly ground black pepper

Set a large pot of boiling water over a high heat, then add the pasta and cook according to the packet instructions.

While the pasta cooks, start making the crumbs. Roughly break up the bread and add to a food processor pot along with one of the garlic cloves. Whizz until all the bread has broken into little crumbs, some chunkier bits are good. Then set a non-stick saucepan on the hob over a medium-low heat and add the butter and oil to melt. Tip in the breadcrumbs and add the thyme, sesame seeds and garlic granules, then cook for 5–8 minutes, stirring often until the crumbs have turned golden and crisp.

While everything cooks, make the hummus. Rinse the butter beans and add to the food processor, along with the lemon juice, remaining garlic clove, roughly chopped, black pepper and sesame oil. Whizz for 3–4 minutes until completely smooth. You may need to scrape down the sides a few times, but keep going until the mixture is very smooth. To help it along, add a ladle of the pasta cooking water. Transfer to a large mixing bowl ready for the pasta.

Once the pasta is done, reserve a little of the cooking water in a mug, then drain before adding the cooked pasta to the butter bean hummus immediately while still piping hot. Use two spoons to toss the pasta into the hummus to coat evenly, adding a little of your reserved pasta water to loosen the consistency if necessary.

Serve in bowls with a generous helping of breadcrumbs on each portion. And a little salt and pepper on top for the adult bowls too.

 **Love your leftovers**

Store the leftover crumbs in an airtight container at room temperature for 2 days, and the pasta covered in the fridge for up to 3 days. Reheat in a frying pan with an extra splash of water until bubbling and piping hot throughout. This dish is not suitable for freezing.

# Korean Garlic Bread

Okay, full disclosure, this recipe is *loosely* based on the gorgeous Korean dish and I've simplified it here to keep the costs down, but oh my it's yummy. To prewarn you, we love garlic, so it's packed in here, but if you fancy a subtler, milder taste, just add half the amount of fresh garlic to your bake.

 **Makes 2**

**Prep 10 mins, Bake 12-13 mins**

### Ingredients

120g (⅔ cup) soft cream cheese*, at room temperature

40g (1½oz) Cheddar cheese, grated*

2 soft round bread rolls*

#### From the pantry

½ tsp dried parsley (optional)

1 tsp garlic granules

1 garlic clove, crushed

oil for cooking, preferably garlic-infused oil or sunflower oil

freshly ground black pepper

Preheat the oven to 200°C fan (220°C/425°F/Gas 7) and line a baking sheet.

In a bowl, add the cream cheese, 30g (1oz) of the grated cheese, parsley if using, garlic granules, crushed garlic and a good grinding of black pepper. Mix it all up very well and set aside.

Take a bread roll and cut a slit down the centre, but don't cut through, leave approx. 1.5cm (⅝in) still attached at the bottom. Now turn the roll and cut another slit, leaving the bottom attached too to form a cross. Now rotate again and cut slits between these cross lines, again don't cut all the way through the roll. You'll be left with 8 sections like a cake that has been cut (almost) into slices. Repeat with the other roll.

Now take a dinner knife and divide the cream cheese mixture in half. Use half the mixture for each roll, spreading the mixture between the slits, trying to fill as deep down as possible without tearing the roll in half. Once all are filled, use your hands to gently press the roll together to form a round bun again, then place on the prepared baking sheet. Drizzle the bread tops with a little garlic-infused oil, then in the centre add a touch more grated cheese.

Bake for 12–13 minutes until the cheese on top has turned golden and the bread edges are crispy. You can also air-fry these at 200°C (400°F) for 10 minutes until golden all over.

Allow to cool for a few minutes before digging in alongside your favourite soup.

 **Love your leftovers**

Leftovers will keep in an airtight container at room temperature for 24 hours. Enjoy cold or reheat for 5 minutes in the oven at 180°C fan (200°C/400°F/Gas 6) or air fryer at 180°C (350°F).

**Leftover** soup will keep for 3 days in an airtight container in the fridge or freeze for up to 3 months. Defrost thoroughly and reheat in a saucepan until piping hot, adding more water as it will thicken. The toast is best enjoyed fresh.

# Cauli and Broccoli Cheese Soup with Garlic Toast

GF*

EF

DF*

V

Vg*

I always add broccoli to my cauliflower cheese to pair with our Sunday roasts, so when I decided to turn it into a simple midweek soup for dinner, we loved it in my house! Sourdough bread is best for the toast, but any bread will work.

 **Makes 6 medium bowls**

 **Prep 5 mins, Cook 20 mins**

## Ingredients

400g (14oz/1 small head) cauliflower

200g (7oz/½ head) broccoli

350g (12oz) all-rounder potatoes

130g (4½oz) strong Cheddar cheese*, grated

### From the pantry

4 thick slices of bread*

4 tsp soft unsalted butter or spread*

3 large garlic cloves, peeled

1 low-salt vegetable stock cube*

freshly ground black pepper

Cut the broccoli and cauliflower into florets and add to a large saucepan. Peel the potatoes and cut into eighths. Add these to the pan too, along with 2 of the garlic cloves, peeled but left whole, the crumbled stock cube and a good grinding of black pepper. Add 1 litre (4¼ cups) of boiling water from the kettle, stir and put over a high heat with the lid. Once boiling, turn the heat to medium and let it simmer for 15–20 minutes until the potatoes are tender when you insert a knife.

Meanwhile, after approx. 10 minutes, make the toasts. Spread both sides of each piece of bread thinly with the butter or spread, then heat a large heavy-based frying pan. Add the bread, in batches if the pan isn't large enough, and toast over a high heat for 1–2 minutes on each side, being careful not to let it burn.

Cut the remaining garlic clove in half on a diagonal so you expose a large surface area. As soon as the toast comes out of the pan, rub the toast with the garlic clove while the bread is still hot. It will instantly take on a little of the garlic, not too strong but a delicious hum of additional flavour. I like to rub both sides but you can do just one if you wish. Set aside; don't worry if it goes cold, we enjoy it this way, or you can place in a low oven to keep warm.

Once the veggies and potatoes are soft, take the pan off the heat and use a stick blender to blend until smooth. We like ours thick so leave as is, but you can top up with some boiling water from the kettle, a little at a time, until you reach your desired consistency.

Now, finally, add the grated cheese, reserving a little for serving, and stir it into the hot soup to melt. Serve up into bowls with a piece of garlic toast on the side for dunking.

If serving to little ones, keep the soup thick to serve on loaded spoons and serve the toast in finger strips for dunking. Alternatively, water it down to serve in a sippy cup. Adults, you may like to add some salt and additional pepper to your portion.

# Tofu, Sesame and Soy Noodles

A super simple noodle dish, using minimal ingredients for a delicious fakeaway at home on a budget. This recipe uses tofu as the protein but you can easily swap it for plant-based meat, or if you do eat meat you can use steak strips or chicken pieces too. Delicious with prawns as well!

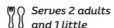 **Serves 2 adults and 1 little**

 **Prep 10 mins, Cook 10 mins**

### Ingredients

125g (4½oz) egg noodles*

280g (9½oz) block of firm tofu

2 spring onions (scallions), finely sliced

½ large red pepper, sliced into strips

3 large chestnut or button mushrooms, thickly sliced

### From the pantry

4 tbsp cornflour (cornstarch)

1 tbsp sunflower or garlic-infused oil

2–3 tbsp low-salt soy sauce*

1 tbsp sesame oil

1 tsp garlic purée or 2 garlic cloves, crushed

Set a pan of boiling water over a high heat and cook the noodles according to the packet instructions. Once done, drain in a colander and leave on the side until needed.

Pat the tofu dry using kitchen paper and cut either into 8 cubes or into chunky strips, strips are easier for little fingers to hold. Add to a bowl along with 2 tablespoons of cornflour and coat all sides of the tofu in the flour. Set aside.

Heat a large non-stick frying pan or wok over a very high heat. Add the sunflower or garlic-infused oil, then place the tofu pieces in the hot pan, ensuring they aren't touching. Cook for 8 minutes, turning the pieces often so they brown on all sides.

While the tofu cooks, make the sauce in a small bowl by mixing together the soy sauce, sesame oil, garlic purée, 2 tablespoons of cornflour and 70ml (⅓ cup) of cold water.

Once the tofu has crisped up and turned a little brown on all sides, remove from the pan and set aside. Using the residual oil left in the pan, add the mushrooms and sauté for 2 minutes, then add the peppers and cook together for 2–4 minutes until they are as soft as you wish. Add the spring onions and toss the pan well.

Rinse the noodles under a running tap and separate them, shaking the colander well to remove the excess water. Add the noodles to the pan and cook for a further minute to warm up again. Now add back in the tofu and pour over the sauce, giving it a stir before you pour it into the pan to ensure the cornflour is mixed into the liquid properly.

Stir-fry and toss for 1–2 minutes, coating everything very well in the sauce. Once warm, the sauce should turn thick and glossy. Ensure the noodles are piping hot, adding a splash of water to the pan if you feel the sauce has become too thick. Serve straight away, adults adding some chilli oil and more sauce if you wish.

If you're swapping your proteins, coat in cornflour as above, but cook according to the ingredient you have, for example, prawns for 2–3 minutes until they are pink, steak for 2–3 minutes until just seared.

# Slow cooker

# Chicken Kyiv Pasta

This pasta is inspired by the 1970s classic, bringing all the flavours of a chicken Kyiv to a delicious one-pot meal.

 **2 adults and 2 littles**

**Prep 5 mins, Cook 4-7 hours**

## Ingredients

600g (1lb 5oz) boneless, skinless chicken thighs

1 large courgette (zucchini), finely grated

150g (¾ cup) cream cheese*

### From the pantry

3 garlic cloves, puréed or grated

25g (1½ tbsp) unsalted butter*

1 low-salt chicken stock cube*

150ml (⅔ cup) milk* 250g (9oz) pasta*

freshly ground black pepper

To a slow-cooker pot, add the chicken thighs, grated courgette, garlic, a good grinding of black pepper and the butter.

Boil the kettle and dissolve the stock cube in 550ml (2½ cups) of water, then add this to the chicken too. Stir really well, so the chicken has unravelled and is submerged under the stock, then pop the lid on and cook on HIGH for 3 hours, or LOW for 6 hours.

Once the chicken is soft and tender, in a separate bowl, add the cream cheese and milk and stir until well combined. Pour this into the slow cooker, along with the uncooked pasta. Stir really well, slightly squashing each piece of chicken with the wooden spoon to help it break up a little.

Put the lid back on and cook on HIGH for 40 minutes or LOW for 1 hour. Once done, stir really well and then put the lid on to stand for 5 minutes before stirring again and serving.

**Tip** For an even creamier cheesier texture, add 50g (1¾oz) of grated Cheddar* once all is cooked before leaving to stand for 5 minutes. Once done it will have melted into the sauce for a delicious extra flavour.

**No slow cooker?** Sear the chicken in a large saucepan in a little oil until golden on the outside, no need to be cooked through. Then add the remaining ingredients, except the pasta, cream cheese and milk. Cover and simmer over a low heat for 30–40 minutes until the chicken is tender. Now add the pasta, cream cheese and milk, with a splash of water if you feel like it needs it. Cover and simmer for 12-15 minutes over a medium heat, stirring often, until the pasta is cooked, and the sauce is creamy.

## ♡ Love your leftovers

If you have any left, pour into an ovenproof dish and store in the fridge for 2 days or the freezer for 1 month. Defrost thoroughly, then add a splash more milk to the base of the dish, top with grated cheese and bake at 200°C fan (220°C/425°F/Gas 7) for 15–20 minutes until golden and crisp on top and piping hot throughout.

# Spanish Chicken and Sweetcorn Stew

GF*

EF

DF

Soft tender chicken, sweet corn kernels, in a delicious smoky paprika sauce. Fantastic paired with potatoes, pasta or rice, or just on its own with little soft flatbreads for dunking.

 **Serves 3 adults and 2 littles**

 **Prep 5 mins, Cook 3–6 hours**

## Ingredients

500g (1lb 2oz) boneless chicken thighs

300g (10½oz) frozen sweetcorn kernels

### From the pantry

1 x 400g (14oz) can of cannellini or haricot beans in water

500g (1lb 2oz) passata (strained tomatoes)

3 tsp smoked paprika

1 low-salt chicken stock cube*

2 large garlic cloves, crushed

good grinding of black pepper

Rinse the beans in the sink, then add to a flat-bottomed bowl and mash using a potato masher. It doesn't need to be smooth, but make sure you smush every bean so none are left whole. Add them to the slow-cooker pot along with the rest of the ingredients. Half-fill the passata container with cold water from the tap, swilling out any left in the corners and add this too.

Give it all a really good stir, ensuring the chicken is flattened out too. Then put the lid on and cook on HIGH for 3 hours or on LOW for 5–6 hours until the chicken is very tender.

Whole sweetcorn kernels do not pose a choking risk to weaning babies, so these are fine to serve whole from 6 months old, but if you're worried, you can blend the sauce a little, keeping some chunks of chicken aside for baby for finger foods. Adults, add a good sprinkling of salt to your portion and some chilli if you fancy it.

 **Love your leftovers**

Leftovers will keep for 2 days in an airtight container in the fridge or freeze for up to 3 months. Defrost thoroughly, then either reheat in a saucepan or microwave for 3–4 minutes until piping hot throughout.

**Don't have a
slow cooker?**
Add all the ingredients to
a large, lidded saucepan
and cook over a low heat for
40 minutes, stirring often.
Top up with more water if
needed as it cooks.

# Garlic Teriyaki Chicken Noodles

GF*

EF*

DF

Loosely based on a traditional teriyaki sauce, this recipe calls for much less salty soy sauce and sugar, making it perfect for all the family, but trust me, you'll love this one just as much as your local takeaway. I love to cook this for my Nina, who isn't a fan of mushrooms, as they kind of melt into the sauce and aren't as noticeable in the finished dish.

**Serves 2 adults and 2 littles**

**Prep 10 mins, Cook 3 hours**

## Ingredients

150g (5½oz) button or chestnut mushrooms

350g (12oz) boneless, skinless chicken thighs

200g (7oz) egg noodles*

### From the pantry

1 low-salt chicken stock cube*

3 tbsp very low salt soy sauce*

1 tbsp sesame oil

1 tbsp honey or sugar (optional)*

3 large garlic cloves

50g (3½ tbsp) cornflour (cornstarch)

freshly ground black pepper

Boil the kettle and crumble the stock cube into the slow-cooker pot. Measure out 300ml (1¼ cups) of boiling water and add to the stock cube, stirring to help it dissolve.

Use a box grater to grate the mushrooms or chop finely using a knife. Add to the slow cooker too, along with the chicken, soy sauce, sesame oil, a good grinding of black pepper and honey or sugar, if using.

On the fine side of the box grater, finely grate the garlic, you should be left with a generous tablespoon of garlic, add this to the slow cooker too.

Finally, measure the cornflour into a bowl, then add 50ml (scant ¼ cup) of cold water from the tap, stir to make a smooth slurry, and pour into the pot. Give everything a really good stir, ensure the chicken is lying flat and submerged in the liquid, then put the lid on and cook on HIGH for 3 hours.

**Recipe continues on page 192**

**No slow cooker?**
Sear the chicken in a large saucepan in a little oil until golden on the outside, no need to be cooked through. Then add the remaining ingredients, pop the lid on and simmer for 30–40 minutes until the chicken is tender and the sauce has thickened. Keep an eye on it – if the sauce is drying up, add a splash more water.

Once done, take the lid off and give it all a good stir to break up the chicken a little. The sauce should be dark and thickened and the meat falling apart easily.

If you would prefer a thicker sauce, mix 1 tablespoon of cornflour with a splash of water and stir into the sauce. Put the lid on and cook on HIGH until your noodles are ready. But do note when you add the noodles it will feel like a thicker sauce.

Cook the noodles according to the packet instructions, then drain very well to avoid thinning down the sauce too much. Add to the chicken, stir well using tongs and serve.

Delicious with a scattering of sesame seeds and broccoli on the side, or adults you can add some chilli sauce and more soy sauce if you wish.

 **Love your leftovers**

Leftovers will keep in an airtight container for 4 days. I like to pop these in the air fryer for 5 minutes to reheat or you can enjoy cold. They will also freeze well for up to 2 months. Defrost in the oven from frozen for 8–10 minutes until piping hot throughout.

# Mexican Soup

Fully loaded, this taco-inspired soup is bursting with flavour and goodness. Super easy to whip up, and comforting enough for a cosy winter's day, but easily freshened up for those warmer months with some fresh toppings to enjoy on the side.

**2 adults and 3 littles**

**Prep 5 mins, Cook 3-10 mins**

## Ingredients

500g (1lb 2oz) minced (ground) lean beef* or plant-based mince*

2 small onions

300g (10½oz) frozen sweetcorn

### From the pantry

1 x 400g (14oz) can of kidney beans in water

2 x 400g (14oz) cans of chopped tomatoes

1 low-salt beef or vegetable stock cube*

2 tsp smoked paprika

2 tsp ground cumin

black pepper

3 crushed garlic cloves or 3 tsp garlic granules

### To serve

sour cream or yogurt*

bread or tortilla chips*

grated cheese*

Add the beef to a large non-stick frying pan set over a high heat. Break it up and cook for 5 minutes. You can either leave the meat in decent-sized chunks (around a 50p coin size) or break up the meat very small with a wooden spoon as it browns.

Meanwhile, prepare the rest of the soup. Drain and rinse the kidney beans and add to the slow cooker. If your little ones are under 2, I recommend smashing them a little to break the beans into smaller pieces. Do this with a potato masher in the slow-cooker pot.

Now add the tomatoes, then fill each empty can with cold water, swilling any residue into the water, and add this to the slow cooker too. Crumble in the stock cube, followed by the remaining ingredients.

Once the mince has browned all over and you see no raw red meat, add this to the slow cooker too, including any juices. Mix everything really well and put the lid on.

This is a great one to have simmering away all day while you're out so cook on LOW for 8–10 hours, or if you need it done quicker, 3–4 hours on HIGH will be fine too.

**Recipe continues on page 194**

Once done, serve as is with some grated cheese on top, and some sour cream if you like. Bread or tortilla chips are great for dunking and scooping.

Adults, give your portion a really good seasoning with salt, and if you're serving to little ones under 12 months, I recommend blending their portion to a chunky texture so it's easier to eat. Or, alternatively, drain the liquid from the soup and serve this in a cup, and the other ingredients on the side with a spoon.

**No slow cooker?**
Brown the mince in a large soup pan first, then add the remaining ingredients. Pop the lid on, bring the soup to a boil and simmer for 30 minutes before serving.

 *Love your leftovers*

Leftovers will keep for 3 days in the fridge or freeze for up to 3 months. Defrost and reheat until piping hot in the microwave or saucepan.

# Dump and Bake Bread

A take on the slow-cooker favourite dump cake, I give you dump and bake bread! This is the perfect thing to easily whip up when you don't have any bread in, delicious for an open sarnie, or serve warm with your favourite soup.

GF*

EF

DF*

V

Vg*

 **Makes 1 medium loaf**

 **Prep 5 minutes, Cook 2 hours 15 minutes**

### Ingredients

100g (3½oz) Cheddar cheese*, grated, plus extra for sprinkling

200ml (1 cup) Greek yogurt*

### From the pantry

500g plain (all-purpose) flour*

20g (1½ tbsp) baking powder*

2 tsp garlic granules

200ml (scant 1 cup) milk*

Take a piece of non-stick baking paper which is large enough to fill your slow-cooker pot. Scrunch it up into a bowl in your hands then unravel it, this will make it easier to mould it into shape in your slow-cooker pot.

Now, in a mixing bowl, add the flour and baking powder, sifting it if you feel it is clumpy. Mix together well, then add the cheese and garlic granules and stir again. Now measure in the yogurt and milk and stir with a spoon until it clumps together in parts. Tip the entire lot into your slow cooker, then, with one hand, gently press together to form a round loaf, this should only take a couple of seconds.

Flatten with the palm of your hand to around 5cm (2in) thick, then, using a large sharp knife, cut a cross over the entire loaf, cutting halfway through the dough.

Sprinkle a small handful of cheese over the top. Then take 4 sheets of kitchen paper, ensuring they are all still attached. Fold in half so you have 2 layers of 2 sheets, then place over your slow-cooker pot, placing the lid down so that the kitchen paper pokes up all around the lid. This will catch the condensation from the bread, stopping it from going soggy.

Bake on HIGH for 2 hours and 15 minutes. After this time is up, take the lid off, and remove the paper carefully, ensuring any water gathered doesn't fall down onto the loaf. The bread should be a lovely golden brown colour and risen well. Insert a knife into it, if no raw dough comes out onto the blade, it is ready. Remove from the slow cooker, using the paper to lift it up, and allow to cool before slicing when still a touch warm – this is when it's the tastiest in my opinion.

 **Love your leftovers**

Leftovers will keep for 3 days in an airtight container, but like normal bread it will start to go stale after the first day, so is best eaten fresh. You can also freeze it for up to 3 months – freeze in slices, then defrost and warm up in the toaster. Or keep in a large loaf and defrost at room temperature.

**No slow cooker?**
Bake in the oven at
180°C fan (200°C/
400°F/Gas 6) for
30–40 minutes.

# Leek and Potato Soup

Easy to whip up in the morning for a warming and hearty lunch or dinner.

GF*

EF

DF*

V

Vg*

**Makes 6 medium bowls**

**Prep 5 mins, Cook 3-5 hours**

## Ingredients

350g (12oz) all-rounder potatoes

2 medium leeks

2 heaped tbsp full-fat cream cheese or crème fraîche*

### From the pantry

1 low-salt vegetable or chicken stock cube*

2 garlic cloves

250g self-raising flour*

1½ tsp baking powder*

freshly ground black pepper

150ml (⅔ cup) milk*

Peel and cube the potatoes into 2cm (¾in) chunks and add to the slow cooker.

Slice the leeks down the centre, keeping the stalk attached, then run water from the tap through the leeks with the open side down, so that any dirt washes away. Then roughly chop the leeks into chunks, discarding the stalk and adding to the slow cooker.

Crumble in the stock cube, peel the garlic and chop in half, then add to the slow cooker along with a generous grinding of black pepper.

Measure the milk into a jug and add to the slow cooker, then measure in 1 litre (4¼ cups) of water, adding this too. Give everything a really good stir, then put the lid on. Cook on HIGH for 3 hours or on LOW for 5 hours. It'll be done when the potatoes are fork tender.

Blitz to a smooth consistency using a stick blender. Now add the cream cheese and stir to melt into the soup. You can thin it down if you wish with a little more milk.

Serve as is with a little crusty buttered bread for dunking.

 **Love your leftovers**

Leftovers will keep for 2 days in the fridge or freeze for 1 month. Defrost thoroughly and reheat in a saucepan until bubbling and piping hot throughout.

**No slow cooker?**
Add all the ingredients to a large saucepan and simmer for 20 minutes until the potatoes and leeks are tender, then blend before adding the cream cheese.

# Banana Peach Cake

GF*
DF*
V

This cake is giving serious comforting vibes. Moist, sweet and really easy to put together. A great one to get baking before you head out for a walk and return to the best afternoon treat.

 **Serves 8-10**

 **Prep 10 mins,
Cook 2-2½ hours**

## Ingredients

1 x 415g (14½oz) can of peach slices in juice

3 medium ripe bananas

1 x 410g (14½oz) can of unsweetened evaporated milk*

70g (⅓ cup) light soft brown or caster sugar (superfine) (optional)

### From the pantry

100g (scant ½ cup) unsalted butter*, melted, plus extra (optional) for greasing

2 eggs

2 tsp vanilla extract

450g (3⅓ cups) self-raising flour*

1 heaped tsp baking powder*

2 tsp ground cinnamon

Cut a piece of non-stick baking paper to fit neatly in the base of your slow cooker. A large slow cooker works best for this recipe, roughly 6.5 litres (27⅓ cups), but slightly smaller will also work. Grease the sides of the slow-cooker bowl if it's not non-stick.

Add the canned peaches evenly to the base of the slow cooker, reserving the liquid for later.

In a mixing bowl, mash the bananas, then add the butter, eggs, evaporated milk, vanilla extract and sugar, if using. Whisk very well until fully combined. Add 80ml (⅓ cup) of the reserved peach juices, mix again, then add the remaining dry ingredients.

Stir well to form a smooth, lump-free batter, but be sure to avoid overworking it. Pour the cake batter into the slow cooker, in a thin even layer over the top of the fruit, to avoid moving the peaches too much and so they stay evenly distributed at the base of the slow cooker.

Take 4 pieces of kitchen paper, all still attached on one long sheet, then fold over in half so you have two layers of two, and place this over the top of the slow cooker, followed by the lid. Gently pull the sides of the kitchen paper to ensure it is not sagging in the middle. If your kitchen paper is on the thin side, I recommend using 8 pieces, to help soak up as much extra liquid as possible. You can also use a tea towel here, as long as you haven't used too strong smelling washing detergents.

Cook on HIGH for 2–2½ hours, depending on the size and shape of your slow cooker. Check after 2 hours and insert a knife into the centre; if it comes out clean with no raw batter stuck to it, then it should be ready. Turn off the slow cooker and let the cake stand with the lid off for 5 minutes. Run a spatula around the edges of the cake, then place a board or serving plate over the slow cooker and turn it all over using oven gloves, as the slow-cooker pot will be very hot. Allow the turned out cake to cool until just warm, then serve up in slices and enjoy.

**Leftovers** will store in an airtight container for 2–3 days or you can freeze for up to 3 months, defrosting at room temperature.

# Cajun Pork and Mash

Cook your meat and potatoes in one pot so that those meat juices and spices flavour the mash deliciously. Plus, there's some hidden veggies in those spuds too, win-win!

GF*

EF

DF

 **Serves 2 adults and 2 littles**

 **Prep 10 mins, Cook 3½–6 hours**

## Ingredients

4 pork shoulder steaks

800g (1lb 12oz) all-rounder potatoes

400g (14oz) swede, peeled and diced

### From the pantry

sunflower oil, for cooking

1 low-salt chicken stock cube*

1 tsp ground cumin

2 tsp smoked paprika

2 tsp garlic granules

freshly ground black pepper

**No slow cooker?**
Pop all the ingredients into a casserole dish and bake in the oven, covered, at 160°C fan (180°C/350°F/Gas 4) for 2 hours.

Heat a large frying pan over a high heat with a little oil. Then sear the pork for a minute on each side, working in 2 batches to avoid overcrowding the pan. You want to quickly seal the meat to keep in the juices and flavour, but not cook it all the way through. Then transfer to a plate and set aside.

Peel and cube the potatoes into approx. 2cm (¾in) chunks, then cut the turnip a little smaller. Add to your slow-cooker pot along with the crumbled stock cube.

In a small bowl, add the cumin, paprika, garlic granules and a good grinding of black pepper and stir to combine. Add half of this mixture to the potatoes and turnips and stir to combine. Then measure 400ml (1⅔ cups) of water in a jug and add to the frying pan you seared the pork steaks in, with the heat off. Briefly stir to dissolve any cooking juices into the liquid, then pour this over the potatoes. Stir very well and even out the potatoes and turnip.

With the remaining spice mix, sprinkle half over the top of the pork steaks, then place these spiced-side down in the slow cooker on the potatoes, avoiding overlapping the meat. They won't be submerged in the liquid, but that's fine. Then sprinkle over the remaining spice mix and pop the lid of the slow cooker on.

Cook on HIGH for 3½ hours or LOW for 6 hours. Once done, the meat will be very tender and the potatoes cooked through. Carefully transfer the pork to a serving plate, trying to keep each piece whole, and spoon over a little juice on each one to keep it moist and warm. Now, using a potato masher, mash the spuds and turnip to a smooth purée before serving up alongside the pork.

 **Love your leftovers**

Leftovers will keep for 2 days in the fridge. Reheat the pork at 180°C fan (200°C/400°F/Gas 6) in an ovenproof dish with a little dash of water, covered with foil, for 15–20 minutes until piping hot throughout. The mash can be microwaved for 3 minutes, or reheat in a saucepan with a little more water too. You can also freeze this dish for up to 1 month, defrosting thoroughly and reheating as above.

For little ones, cut
the pork into finger
strips and serve the mash
on a preloaded spoon.
Adults, add a little salt
to your portion
if you wish.

# Slow-cooker Butter Chicken Pasta

This is a bit of a cuisine mash-up, but my goodness it is delicious!

 GF*

 EF

DF*

 **Serves 2 adults and 2 littles**

**Prep 5 mins, Cook 3-5½ hours**

## Ingredients

200ml (1 cup) Greek yogurt*

1 large onion

500g (1lb 2oz) boneless, skinless chicken thighs or breast, cut into large chunks

### From the pantry

2 tsp crushed garlic

1½ tsp ground cumin

4 tsp smoked paprika

2 tsp mild garam masala

1 low-salt chicken stock cube*

2 tbsp tomato purée (paste) (optional)

200g (7oz) pasta* (I prefer orzo)

freshly ground black pepper

To the slow-cooker pot, add the yogurt, garlic, cumin, paprika, garam masala and a generous grinding of black pepper. Stir very well, then add the onion either finely diced with a knife or I like to grate mine on a box grater for minimal "onion bits". Add the chicken to the pot too.

Finally, dissolve the stock cube in 400ml (1⅔ cups) of water and the tomato purée, stirring very well, then add this to the slow cooker too, giving everything one final stir to combine. Pop the lid on and cook for 2½ on HIGH or 4–5 hours on LOW.

Once done, the chicken should be very tender, give it a stir, then add the pasta and mix in to coat all the pasta pieces in the sauce. Pop the lid back on and cook for a further 25–30 minutes on HIGH until the pasta is cooked through.

Serve with a side of greens with the chicken cut into strips or shredded for little ones. Adults you may want to add some salt to your portion too.

**No slow cooker?** Make the chicken curry in a saucepan instead as above and simmer for 20 minutes, ideally sealing the chicken in the pan first before adding the remaining ingredients. Then add the pasta and cook for 10 minutes until soft, you will need to keep topping up with a little more water as it evaporates in the pan.

**Tip** For the chicken, I like to use thigh meat as it's the juiciest, but breast will also work.

♡ *Love your leftovers*

Leftovers will store in an airtight container in the fridge for 3 days or freeze for up to 3 months. Allow to thaw in the fridge, then reheat in a saucepan until piping hot throughout, you may need to add a splash of water to help loosen the sauce.

# Freezer Raid Veg Stew

This a real store-cupboard/freezer winner for when you don't have much in. I always have a packet of chorizo in my fridge, but if you don't or you don't eat meat, then feel free to just leave it out. Equally feel free to swap out the veg for what you have in, this is a very forgiving recipe and a great one for adapting.

**Serves 3 adults and 3 littles**

**Prep 5 mins, Cook 3-8 hours**

### Ingredients

75g (2½oz) mild Spanish chorizo*

250g (9oz) frozen green beans

250g (9oz) frozen peas

.............

### From the pantry

1 x 400g (14oz) can of haricot beans in water

1 x 400g (14oz) can of finely chopped tomatoes or passata

300g (10½oz) frozen sweetcorn

4 garlic cloves

1 low-salt chicken or vegetable stock cube*

2 tsp smoked paprika

Rinse the beans and add to the slow cooker along with the tomatoes. Fill the empty tomato can with water from the tap and add this too, followed by all the frozen veg.

Peel the chorizo and cut in half lengthways, then into little half-moon discs. Peel the garlic, but leave it whole or chop very roughly. Add these to the veg, along with a crumbled stock cube and the smoked paprika. Give it a very good stir, pop the lid on and cook on HIGH for 3–4 hours or LOW for 6–8 hours.

Serve in a big bowl with some crusty bread for mopping up all those yummy juices. For little ones under 2, chop the chorizo into smaller pieces for them. If you wish, you can also blend for young newly weaning babies to enjoy on a spoon, or even mix through pasta for a delicious alternative way to enjoy lots of veggies.

**No slow cooker?** Add all the ingredients to a large saucepan and simmer for 30–40 minutes until everything is tender; you may need to top up with more water as it evaporates.

**Love your leftovers**

Leftovers will store in the fridge for 2 days or freeze for 3 months. Reheat in a saucepan until bubbling and piping hot throughout.

# Sunday Dinner Pork Belly

Pork is one of the cheaper meat options for a Sunday roast, and great for serving a large crowd. Super soft juicy tender meat with gorgeous pork crackling.

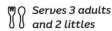
*Serves 3 adults and 2 littles*

*Prep 10 mins, Cook 2-3 hours*

## Ingredients

800g (1lb 12oz) slab of pork belly with the rind still attached

### From the pantry

1 tsp peppercorns from the grinder

6 garlic cloves

1 tsp oil

1 tsp mixed dried herbs

salt

*Love your leftovers*

Leftovers will keep in the fridge for 3 days, cut into chunks and fry in a little oil and spices for a delicious taco filling.

Bring the meat up to room temperature while you pat the skin dry with some kitchen paper. Add the pork, flat and unravelled, to a slow-cooker pot, with the fatty skin-side facing up. Then add the peppercorns and garlic, no need to peel the cloves. Ensure that you place them down the sides of the pork and not on the skin.

Then add enough cold water to just cover the meat, but not the fatty line under the skin. It's important that you don't splash the water onto the skin, and gently pour it into the slow cooker down the sides so it doesn't touch the skin, to keep it as dry as possible for a crispier skin later.

Place the lid on and cook for 1 hour 40 minutes–2 hours on HIGH until the meat is tender. You can also cook for 4 hours on LOW if you'd prefer.

Take a large piece of cooking foil and lay it over a baking sheet. In the centre, add the oil and a sprinkling of herbs, roughly the same size as the meat. Then carefully remove the meat from the slow cooker using a fish slice. Let any juice drop into the slow cooker for a second before transferring the pork over and placing on the herby oil. Fold and roll the excess foil in 4cm (1.5in) sections towards the meat, then scrunch or fold the ends together to form a little open topped box for the pork to sit in, with the fatty skin on top completely exposed. Use kitchen paper to pat the skin dry again, it'll feel sticky to touch, this is what you want. Add a liberal coating of salt to just the skin, this will really help it crisp up. If you're serving to little ones, don't worry – it will just be the crackling for adults that is salty, the soft meat underneath will be untouched.

Allow it to sit to one side for 15 minutes so the skin can dry out further, and preheat the grill to 180°C.

Once hot, grill the meat directly under the heat for 20 minutes until the crackling has turned crispy and bubbled up. Keep an eye on it, and rotate the meat if necessary for an even grilling. Serve in slices, with the fatty line removed for little ones.

**No slow cooker?** Make the foil boat for the raw pork with oil, herbs and pepper to marinate. Pat the skin dry and salt the top. Cook at 140°C fan (160°C/325°F/Gas 3) for 1 hour, then turn the heat up to 220°C fan (240°C/475°F/Gas 9) and cook until you have delicious crispy crackling.

# Something
# sweet

# Ginger Oat Flapjacks

Soft moreish flapjacks, flavoured with comforting ginger and little chocolate chips, which you can leave out if serving to newly weaning little ones.

**Makes
16 squares**

**Prep 10 mins,
Bake 18-22 mins,
plus cooling**

## Ingredients

3 ripe bananas, approx.
300g (10½oz)

100g (3½oz) your choice
of chocolate chips
(optional)*

### From the pantry

80g (⅓ cup) unsalted
butter*

2–4 tsp ground ginger

1 tsp vanilla extract

20–40g (2–3½ tbsp) light
soft brown sugar
(optional)

350g (3½ cups) porridge
oats*

Preheat the oven to 180°C fan (200°C/400°F/Gas 6) and line a 23cm (9in) square cake tin with non-stick baking paper.

Add the butter to a microwaveable bowl, cover and melt for 1 minute.

To a large mixing bowl, add the peeled bananas and mash with the back of a fork. Add the ground ginger, vanilla extract, sugar, if using, and melted butter and stir well. Pour in the oats and mix really well so that the oats are completely coated in the mixture.

Stir in the chocolate chips, if using, then tumble the mixture into your prepared tin. Level out and press into all the corners using the back of a tablespoon, pressing down to a very even flat and smooth surface. Make sure the edges are not raised too.

Bake for 18–22 minutes until browned on top. Remove the flapjack slab from the tin using the baking paper and place on a cooling rack to cool for 20–30 minutes before slicing. Don't attempt to slice too early as it will crumble. Cut into 16 squares and enjoy.

## ♡ Love your leftovers

These flapjacks will last for 5 days in an airtight container at room temperature. You can also freeze them for 3 months, defrosting at room temperature and enjoying fresh. They're great for lunchboxes as they should defrost by lunchtime if packed in the morning.

# Low-sugar Lemon Shortbread

 GF*

 EF

 DF*

V

Vg*

Crumbly and crisp, this classic recipe is adapted to be lower in sugar than standard recipes, but you can use as much or little as you prefer, depending on your little one's age. A great recipe for all the family, with just five simple ingredients, this is cheap and easy to whip up.

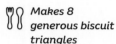 **Makes 8 generous biscuit triangles**

**Prep 5 mins, Bake 25-30 mins**

## Ingredients

zest of 1 large unwaxed lemon

### From the pantry

150g (⅔ cup) chilled unsalted butter*, cubed (see Note)

15–35g caster sugar (superfine)

170g (1¼ cups) plain (all-purpose) flour*

1 tsp vanilla extract

Preheat the oven to 180°C fan (200°C/400°F/Gas 6).

Add the cubed butter, sugar, lemon zest and vanilla to a processor and whizz until well combined. Now add the flour and whizz until it clumps together, this may take a minute or so. If you feel it is not coming together, add 1 tablespoon of lemon juice from your zested lemon to help it bind.

If you don't have a food processor, rub the butter into the flour as if you're making scones, then stir in the remaining ingredients and clump the dough together using your hands.

Tip the dough out onto a clean work surface and press to form a patty shape, then using your hands or a rolling pin, flatten to form a circle approx 1.5cm (⅝in) in thickness. Use a thin spatula to transfer to a lined baking tray, then cut into 8 triangles, no need to separate them. Prick with a fork all over, then pop into the oven.

Bake for 25–30 minutes until golden on the edges. As soon as it comes out of the oven, score over the triangle lines, which will have faded now. Allow to cool completely before enjoying, they're delicious slightly warm but will be very crumbly until they cool.

**Note** If you're opting for dairy-free butter, try to find a version that is firmer and comes in a block rather than soft and spreadable, as this will blend better.

 **Love your leftovers**

Store in an airtight tin for up to 3 weeks. If you'd like to freeze, I recommend freezing the unbaked dough in a log shape, wrapped in cling film or non-stick baking paper. Then thaw for a few moments before slicing into rounds and baking at 180°C fan (200°C/400°F/ Gas 6) for approx. 15 minutes.

These are deliciously crumbly, but if you'd prefer a firmer texture, add 20g (¾oz) more sugar.

# Leftover Rice Pudding

I don't know about you, but I can't seem to ever cook just the right amount of rice for dinner, I always have some left over. So, I started to think about what I can do with the leftovers, and this rice pudding has to be one of our favourite solutions! Only use rice that has been cooled quickly and refrigerated within the hour, or rice you have just cooked for dinner.

GF

EF

DF*

V

Vg*

**Serves 1 adult and 1 little**

**Prep 3 mins, Cook 10-17 mins**

## Ingredients

300g (1⅔ cups) cooked cooled rice (long or short grain)

2 handfuls of frozen sweet cherries (optional)

### From the pantry

1 tsp vanilla extract

1–2 tbsp sugar or honey* (optional)

250ml (generous 1 cup) milk*

Measure the rice, vanilla, sugar (or honey), if using, and milk into a medium non-stick saucepan.

Set over a medium-high heat and simmer for 10–15 minutes until thickened. Keep an eye on it, don't let it boil over and turn the heat down if you feel like it's cooking too vigorously. Stir often to help it turn creamy.

Once all the milk has been absorbed and you have a creamy rice pudding, you can serve straight away, but I like to add a couple of handfuls of frozen cherries and cook for a further 2 minutes until defrosted. Serve in a bowl, mashing the cherries down for little ones under 1.

 **Love your leftovers**

This dish is best served fresh and will not keep for more than 6 hours. Not suitable for freezing.

You can use any fresh or frozen fruit here, strawberries work beautifully.

# Chocolate and Ginger Traybake

Moist sponge with flavours of comforting ginger and chocolate. Enjoy on its own or with a sweetened honey yogurt on top.

 **Makes 10 slices**

 **Prep 15 mins,
Bake 22-25 mins**

## Ingredients

2 very ripe bananas

50–90g (¼–scant ½ cup) light soft brown sugar

50g (½ cup) cocoa powder

160ml (¾ cup) thick Greek yogurt* (optional)

### From the pantry

3 eggs

120g (½ cup) unsalted butter*, melted

200g (1½ cups) self-raising flour*

4 tsp ground ginger

1 tsp baking powder*

2 tbsp honey (optional)

Preheat the oven to 180°C fan (200°C/400°F/Gas 6)  and grease and line a 23cm (9in) square cake tin or rectangular tin of similar dimensions.

To a stand mixer with the whisk attachment fitted, add the bananas and whisk for 1–2 minutes until mashed and pale. Then add the eggs and whisk on high speed for 4 minutes until frothy.

Now pour in the melted butter and sugar and whisk again for 1 minute. Remove the whisk, then into a sieve placed over the bowl, measure the flour, ginger, baking powder and cocoa powder. Sift the dry ingredients into the wet, then gently fold it all together using a spatula until fully combined, but be sure to stop mixing once you see it combined to avoid overmixing.

Pour the batter into the prepared tin, level out and bake for 22–25 minutes until an inserted knife comes out clean.

Allow to cool fully before portioning into 10 pieces. Enjoy as is, or mix up an easy honey yogurt to spoon over the top. For little ones under 12 months, serve with plain yogurt as they must not consume honey before 1 year old.

 **Love your leftovers**

Leftovers will store in an airtight container for 3 days, or you can freeze for 3 months, defrosting at room temperature.

# Yogurt Custard Tarts

**GF\***

**DF\***

**V**

A speedy low-sugar take on a traditional custard tart, these have a gorgeous wobble, and a flaky pastry crust. Delicious enjoyed on their own or with your favourite toppings. You could use any of your favourite flavoured yogurts here if you like.

 **Makes 8**

 **Prep 10 mins, Bake 20 mins**

## Ingredients

1 x 320g (11oz) sheet of ready-rolled puff pastry*

280ml (scant 1½ cups) thick Greek yogurt*

### From the pantry

butter*, for greasing

2 eggs

1 tbsp cornflour (cornstarch)

2 tsp vanilla extract

2 tbsp honey or sugar (optional)

 **Love your leftovers**

Leftovers will store in an airtight container in the fridge for 2–3 days. This dish is best enjoyed fresh rather than freezing.

Preheat the oven to 200°C fan (220°C/425°F/Gas 7) and grease a deep 9 or 12-hole muffin tray.

Unroll the pastry sheet, and cut into 8 pieces. Ideally you will have squares, but rectangles will work too. One at a time, add a pastry piece to a hole in the muffin tray, allowing the pastry to crease at the edges, and use your fingers to press the pastry into all the corners. Where the pastry has overlapped, press it against the metal sides so it is the same thickness throughout. Leave the pastry corners overhanging the top of each section, this way there's no pastry waste.

Crack the eggs into a mixing bowl, and whisk well. Use a pastry brush to cover just the top corners of the pastry cases that will be exposed once baked, this helps the pastry get a lovely golden brown colour when baking.

Now, to the remaining whisked egg, add the cornflour, vanilla and honey, if using (if serving to little ones under 1, leave out or replace with sugar). Whisk very well until you have a smooth batter.

Divide the yogurt mixture between the 8 pastry cases, you should be able to fill each with 6–7 tablespoons. Then carefully place the tray in the preheated oven for 20 minutes, reducing the heat to 180°C fan (200°C/400°F/Gas 6) straight away. Once done, the pastry will have puffed up and turned golden, and the custard inside will have risen and cracked at the top. Let the tarts sit in the tin to cool a little for 5 minutes, the custard will sink back down at this stage, then lift out and transfer to a serving plate.

You can top the tarts with your favourite flavours here, we particularly like chocolate shavings, or sliced strawberries, but use any fruit you like, or maybe try some chopped nuts or nut butter, whatever you have in. Adults, you may wish to add a sprinkling of icing (confectioners') sugar to your portion if you prefer a sweeter taste.

# Chocolate Orange Snack Balls

Looking for something to keep the kids sustained until dinner? These little snack balls are so delightful. With fragrant orange, and moreish chocolate flavours, they are perfect as a festive treat, too.

GF*

EF

DF

V

Vg

**Makes 10**

**6 mins**

## Ingredients

1 large orange, washed

100g (⅔ cup) seedless raisins

1 tbsp unsweetened cocoa powder

### From the pantry

100g (1 cup) rolled porridge oats*

2 tbsp desiccated coconut (optional)

Zest the orange and add to a food processor. Then juice the orange too and add this as well. You should get around 75ml (5 tbsp) of juice, so if your orange is much juicier, balance this with a few extra spoonfuls of oats in the next step.

Now add the raisins and measure in the oats, followed by the cocoa powder.

Put the lid on and whizz for 2–3 minutes until all the raisins have broken down and you can see no whole pieces of oats, the mixture should be fairly smooth and no longer lumpy.

Take walnut-sized amounts of the mixture and roll in your hands to form smooth balls. You can now leave as is or roll in desiccated coconut for extra texture.

**Tip** If you're serving to little ones under 18 months, shape the balls into long finger strips instead and set in the fridge so it's easier for them to hold.

 **Love your leftovers**

Store leftovers in an airtight container in the fridge for up to 3 days. Or freeze for up to 4 months. These are great for lunchboxes as they will defrost by lunchtime and keep other items in the lunchbox cold.

# Carrot and Orange Cake Cookies

Half cake, half cookie, 100% delicious!

GF*

EF

DF*

V

Vg*

**Makes 15**

**Prep 10 mins,
Bake 14-16 mins**

## Ingredients

170g (6oz) carrots

1 medium orange,
washed

### From the pantry

120g (½ cup) unsalted
butter*, cubed

40g (¼ cup) caster
sugar (superfine)
(optional)

250g (2 cups) plain
(all-purpose) flour*,
plus extra (optional)
for dusting

3 tbsp icing
(confectioners')
sugar (optional)

Preheat the oven to 180°C fan (200°C/400°F/Gas 6) and line two baking sheets with non-stick baking paper.

Peel the carrots and chop into rough discs. Then add to a food processor and whizz until the pieces are so small they stick to the sides and there's nothing to blend any more. Scrape down the sides and whizz again. It'll take approx. 30–40 seconds to break down.

Now zest the orange and add to the carrots in the blender (keep the blade in) and measure in the cubed butter, caster sugar if using, and flour. Blend again until the mixture clumps together and you can see no small chunks of butter. Remove the blade and take tablespoon-sized amounts of the mixture and roll into balls in your hands.

The next step is optional, but it gives a delicious sweet crunch to the outside of the cookies. If you're making the cookies for little ones under 2, skip this step if you wish. Add the icing sugar to a small bowl, then as you roll each cookie into a ball, dip it into the icing sugar and coat all over before placing on the prepared baking sheets. Repeat with the remaining mixture, ensuring you place the cookies well apart so that they don't touch as they flatten in the oven. If you find the cookie mixture a little sticky to roll, dust your hands in a little flour and this will help make it easier.

Bake the cookies for 14–16 minutes until they have spread out, puffed up a little and are turning slightly golden in parts. The longer you bake them, the firmer their texture will be.

Allow to cool and enjoy.

### Love your leftovers

Store any leftovers in an airtight container at room temperature for up to 5 days. These cookies will also freeze for up to 3 months. Defrost thoroughly and enjoy cold, or crisp up again in the oven at 180°C fan (200°C/400°F/Gas 6) at for 5 minutes until piping hot throughout.

# Filo Custard Strawberry Slice

Filo pastry soaked in a vanilla-flavoured custard, resulting in a soft, sumptuous filling with a layer of juicy strawberries and crisp filo top. Gorgeous!

GF*

EF

DF*

V

**Makes
8 slices**

**Prep 10 mins,
Bake 30-35 mins**

## Ingredients

300g (10½oz) cottage cheese*

250g (9oz) filo pastry*

250g (9oz) fresh or defrosted frozen strawberries

### From the pantry

50g (scant ¼ cup) unsalted butter*, melted

200ml (scant 1 cup) milk*

2 tsp vanilla extract

2 tbsp cornflour (cornstarch)

40g (¼ cup) caster sugar (superfine) (optional)

Preheat the oven to 180°C fan (200°C/400°F/Gas 6). Brush the base and sides of an approx. 20 x 25cm (8 x 9in) high-sided oven dish with some of the melted butter.

To a blender pot or bowl to use with a stick blender, add the cottage cheese, milk, vanilla, cornflour and sugar, if using. Blend until completely smooth.

Take the filo pastry out of the packet, and set aside two sheets, wrapped in a clean tea towel to stop it from drying out. Then, with the remaining sheets, one by one scrunch them up in your hands and add in a single layer to the oven dish, you should be able to fill the entire dish with scrunched up filo.

Now pour over the custard and use the back of a tablespoon to press the pastry sheets into the custard so they are fully saturated.

Remove the stalks of the strawberries and cut into small diced chunks, or slices. Scatter these evenly across the custardy filo, then layer the two remaining sheets of filo on top, covering the top completely.

Brush all the filo on top liberally with the remaining melted butter, which will help it to crisp up nicely.

Bake for 30–35 minutes until the filo on top has turned golden. Allow the pie to cool for at least 10–15 minutes to ensure it cuts neatly, then use a fish slice to portion up onto serving plates. Adults, if you prefer a sweeter finish, add a sprinkling of icing (confectioners') sugar to your portion.

### ♡ Love your leftovers

Leftovers will store in the fridge for 3 days, the top will become softer as it sits, but this is still delicious or you can crisp it up again in the oven. You can also freeze for 1 month, defrost thoroughly, then reheat in the oven at 180°C fan (200°C/400°F/Gas 6) for 10–15 minutes to crisp up again or until piping hot throughout.

Cottage cheese is packed with protein, perfect for growing little ones, but you can swap for dairy-free yogurt if you have allergies.

# Coconut, Pineapple and Kiwi Ice Pops

Refreshing, creamy, sweet and zingy – perfect on a warm summer's day or when baba is teething badly. And the best thing is, they're made almost entirely of store-cupboard ingredients!

*Makes 8 large lollies*

*Prep 5 mins, freeze at least overnight*

### Ingredients

435g (15½oz) can of pineapple in juice

1 x 400g (14oz) can of coconut milk

2 ripe kiwis

*From the pantry*

1 tsp vanilla extract

To a blender, add the pineapple plus the juice, with the tin of coconut milk, ensuring you scrape out all of the coconut cream. Add the vanilla and blend until very smooth.

Divide the mixture between your moulds, leaving at least a quarter empty for the kiwi. How many lollies you'll get will depend on the size of your lolly moulds.

Leave a couple of spoonfuls of the mixture in the blender jug, then peel the kiwis and add to the blender too. Whizz until completely smooth. Pour this kiwi mixture on top of all the lollies and put the lids on.

Place in the freezer until set, this will likely take a minimum of 6 hours.

♡ *Love your leftovers*

They will last for 3 months in the freezer, perfect for all summer long.

If you have some leftover mixture, it's great made into a smoothie with a little milk.

# Black Forest Pancake Layer Cake

What a showstopper this one is – 20 layers of deliciousness, very low in sugar compared to a usual cake and so satisfying to make. My Nina absolutely loves this one, and we even enjoyed a small slice for brekkie one morning too. It's pancakes after all, right?!

 **Serves 6 adults and 4 littles**

 **Prep 30 mins, Cook 30 mins**

## Ingredients

2 tbsp chocolate shavings or sprinkles (optional)*

35g (2 tbsp) cocoa powder

450g (1lb) frozen sweet dark cherries

600ml (2½ cups) whipping cream*

## From the pantry

350g (2⅔ cups) plain (all-purpose) flour*

5 eggs

3 tsp vanilla extract

700ml (3 cups) milk*

sunflower or vegetable oil, for cooking

40–80g (¼–⅓ cup) caster sugar (superfine), plus 2 tbsp

Add the flour to a large mixing bowl and crack in the eggs. Add 2 teaspoons of vanilla extract, then measure 600ml (2½ cups) of the milk into a measuring jug, reserving the rest for later. Add half the milk to the flour and eggs, then whisk well to remove all lumps, the mixture will be thick and easier to remove any lumps at this stage. Once smooth, gradually pour in the remaining milk until you have a smooth, thin batter.

Take a non-stick frying pan, ideally one that has a 20cm (8in) diameter base. The larger the pan, the bigger the pancake, and this will result in fewer layers, so use a small pan here. Add a small drizzle of oil to the pan set over a high heat. Once the pan is very hot when hovering your hand over it, add around half a large ladleful of batter. Don't add too much as the pancake will be too thick, thin pancakes are best. Once you've added the batter, quickly swill the pan around to spread the batter, before placing the pan back on the heat to cook.

It will take approx. 1 minute before you need to flip, you'll know it's ready because the batter will change from being light in colour to dark, and you will be able to get a thin plastic spatula under the pancake easily. Flip the pancake and cook for another 30–60 seconds until a little browning has appeared on the underside. Transfer to a plate and repeat. I like to have 2 dinner plates on the side, and I alternate which plate I place the hot pancake on, layering around the plates so that they can cool quicker.

Once you have cooked half the batter, you should have 9 or 10 pancakes. Turn the heat off so you can change the colour of your batter for the alternating pancakes. Sift the cocoa powder into a small bowl to remove any lumps, then add 2 tablespoons of caster sugar to offset the cocoa bitterness and stir. Now gradually add the remaining 100ml (scant ½ cup) of milk and stir until you have a smooth paste. Pour this into the remaining pancake batter and mix well.

**Recipe continues on page 232**

This is a good opportunity to clean the frying pan with kitchen paper, then place back on the heat, add a little drizzle of oil and once hot again begin frying the pancakes as before. It's a little harder to tell when the chocolate ones are ready to be flipped, but if you can easily get a spatula underneath they are ready, if not, give them another 30 seconds.

Once all the batter has been used, you should have 10 of each colour pancake, set aside to cool while you make the cream. Add the frozen cherries to a microwaveable bowl, cover and cook on HIGH for 2 minutes to defrost. Move 250g (9oz) of the cherries into another bowl and press out the juice. Then either blend the remaining 200g (7oz) to a purée or mash with a fork. Set aside to cool completely.

In a large bowl or electric mixer, add the cream, your desired amount of caster sugar, depending on your taste and who will be enjoying the cake, and remaining 1 teaspoon of vanilla and whisk to stiff peaks, being careful not to overwhip it. Pour in the cherry purée and whisk until incorporated.

Now it's time to assemble. On your serving plate add your first pancake. Add 1–2 tablespoons of cherry cream and, using the back of the spoon, spread it thinly to reach the edges in an even layer. Now add another pancake of the opposite colour and repeat the process, alternating in pancake flavours until you have a large stack.

Add the remaining cherries to the top of the cake, squeezing out the excess juice first as this slightly splits the cream (if this happens it's completely fine, just give it a little mix with the tip of a spoon and it'll come together again). Top with chocolate shavings or sprinkles and enjoy. If you would like to cream the sides of the cake so it looks more "traditional" add an extra 200ml (scant 1 cup) of cream along with 100g (3½oz) extra of defrosted blitzed cherries so you have plenty to cover the sides too.

For little ones, cut into long cake strips, the layers will come apart when they eat it, it'll be a little messy but lots of yummy fun!

........................................................................

 *Love your leftovers*

This cake lasts for 3 days in the fridge, covered, but is best eaten fresh. Avoid freezing.

This is perfect for birthdays, especially a first birthday milestone, to share with all the family.

# index

**DISCLAIMER**

Those following strict allergen
diets should always check the
packet for guidance about
suitability. The advice given
in this book is based on the
UK national health system
guidance for family eating
and baby weaning, therefore
if you live outside of the UK
and are ever in doubt, refer to
your own country's guidance
for new parents.

**FOOD NOTES**

All-rounder potatoes are
equivalent to all-purpose
varieties in the US – Yukon
Gold is a good example.

Egg sizes given in recipes are
UK. US sizes are as follows:

UK medium = US large

UK large = US extra-large

# publisher's thanks

DK would like to thank Lucy
Upton for dietetic consultancy,
John Friend for proofreading,
Flossy McAslan for food styling,
Lizzie Evans for food styling
assistance, Adam Brackenbury
for image retouching and
Vanessa Bird for the index.

# thank you

This book marks my fifth publication, something I feel incredibly honoured and proud of. As much as I say that I poured everything into writing this book to make it as useful and helpful as it can be for all of you, I couldn't have written it without a huge list of amazing people.

Darryl, my literary agent and friend, thank you for your unwavering support and dedication to help make this book amazing.

Cara and Lucy, thank you for all your dedicated hours on this project, bringing the book together and making it the best it can be!

To Clare, the photos in this book are amazing as always, thank you so much for all your hard work. I love working with you – your calmness and kindness are a joy to be around. Maud, Flossy and Lizzie, thank you for styling the food so beautifully, and Charlie for curating and supplying wonderful props. The book has a wonderful, homely, family feel, exactly how I like to cook for my daughter. Thank you all for helping to portray that so wonderfully.

To the lovely Bess, for your wonderful design eye and direction for this book. Barbara, thank you for making the pages sing so beautifully!

To all the team at DK, Vicky, John, Vanessa, Neha, Umesh, Satish, Raman, Pushpak, Balwant and Malavika, thank you for working so hard to ensure this book is as amazing as it is.

Lucy Upton, thank you for casting your expert nutritionist eye over my words, ensuring all the information is up to date and within guidelines. Your advice is always incredibly valuable, thank you.

Thank you to my friends and family and, of course, my gorgeous darling Nina, who is and forever will be my biggest inspiration. I started to share family-friendly recipes when you were just a tiny baby, and now you're 6 years old and growing into the most caring and courageous person – I feel lucky to call myself your mother and best friend.

And, lastly, I'd like to thank everyone who has bought this book and supported me through the years – making my recipes and feeding your family with them. I wouldn't be writing this if it wasn't for you, so thank you truly.

All my love,

*Rebecca*
*X*

# about the author

Rebecca Wilson is a mum to her 6-year-old daughter Nina, a recipe developer, and founder of her own food channel Rebecca Wilson. Her mission is to make family mealtimes easy for everyone and to show parents and carers that introducing solid foods can be fun, exciting, easy, and most importantly... delicious! She creates recipes for the whole family, so that babies reaching their weaning milestone at six months old can eat the same meal together with their older siblings – and even the adults too!

You can find Rebecca over on her Instagram channel @rebeccawilsonfood where she shares quick and easy meal ideas that are suitable for all the family to enjoy together.

Rebecca's first book, *What Mummy Makes*, published in July 2020 to immediate acclaim and quickly became a chart and Sunday Times No. 1 bestseller. It won the Wordery Food & Drink Book of the Year 2020 and was shortlisted for the 2021 British Book Awards Book of the Year in Non-fiction Lifestyle.

Rebecca has gone on to publish three more bestselling cookery books: *What Mummy Makes Family Meal Planner*, *Family Comforts* and *Fast Family Food*. This is her fifth book.

To find out more head to www.rebeccawilson.com and @rebeccawilsonfood on Instagram.

**DK LONDON**
**Editorial Director** Cara Armstrong
**Project Editor** Lucy Sienkowska
**Senior Designer** Barbara Zuniga
**Production Editor** David Almond
**Senior Production Controller** Stephanie McConnell
**Jacket and Sales Material Coordinator** Emily Cannings
**Art Director** Maxine Pedliham
**Publishing Director** Katie Cowan

**Editorial** Vicky Orchard
**Design and Jacket Design** Bess Daly
**Photography** Clare Winfield
**Food Styling** Maud Eden
**Prop Styling** Charlie Phillips

**DK DELHI**
**Managing Art Editor** Neha Ahuja Chowdhry
**DTP Designers** Umesh Singh Rawat, Satish Gaur, Raman Panwar
**DTP Coordinator** Pushpak Tyagi
**Pre-production Manager** Balwant Singh
**Creative Head** Malavika Talukder

First published in Great Britain in 2024 by
Dorling Kindersley Limited
DK, One Embassy Gardens, 8 Viaduct Gardens,
London, SW11 7BW

The authorised representative in the EEA is
Dorling Kindersley Verlag GmbH. Arnulfstr. 124,
80636 Munich, Germany

A CIP catalogue record for this book
is available from the British Library.
ISBN: 978-0-2416-2488-3

Printed and bound in China

**www.dk.com**

This book was made with Forest
Stewardship Council™ certified
paper – one small step in DK's
commitment to a sustainable future.
**For more information go to
www.dk.com/our-green-pledge**